D1292150

CALLING TO MIND

"*Calling to mind* ——————
  The uncertain times oft varying in their course,
How things still unexpectedly have run,
  As't please the Fates, by their resistless force."
                              —*Michael Drayton*

By the same author:

"Distinctly I Remember"
(Wren Publishing Pty. Ltd., Melbourne, Australia.
Distributors in the U.K.—David & Charles (Publishers) Ltd.)

W. Strang Steel
1890–1897

H. A. Laird
1897–1906

Sir Robert McCracken
1906–1924

Sir James Duncan
1924–1926

B. T. Petley
1926–1930

J. A. Swan
1930–1940

J. K. Michie
1940–1960

P. G. G. Salkeld
1960–1965

W. F. G. Salkeld
1965–1970

THE CHAIRMEN

CALLING TO MIND

BEING SOME ACCOUNT OF THE
FIRST HUNDRED YEARS (1870 TO 1970) OF
STEEL BROTHERS AND COMPANY LIMITED

compiled by
H. E. W. BRAUND, M.B.E., M.C.

from material received from many sources

PERGAMON PRESS
OXFORD · NEW YORK · TORONTO · SYDNEY · PARIS · BRAUNSCHWEIG

U.K.	Pergamon Press Ltd., Headington Hill Hall, Oxford OX3 0BW, England
U.S.A.	Pergamon Press Inc., Maxwell House, Fairview Park, Elmsford, New York 10523, U.S.A.
CANADA	Pergamon of Canada, Ltd., 207 Queen's Quay West, Toronto 1, Canada
AUSTRALIA	Pergamon Press (Aust.) Pty. Ltd., 19a Boundary Street, Rushcutters Bay, N.S.W. 2011, Australia
FRANCE	Pergamon Press SARL, 24 rue des Ecoles, 75240 Paris, Cedex 05, France
WEST GERMANY	Pergamon Press GMbH, D-3300 Braunschweig, Postfach 2923, Burgplatz 1, West Germany

Copyright © 1975 Steel Brothers and Company Ltd.

All Rights Reserved. No part of this publication may be reproduced, stored in a retrieval system or transmitted in any form or by any means: electronic, electrostatic, magnetic tape, mechanical, photocopying, recording or otherwise, without permission in writing from the publishers

First edition 1975

Library of Congress Catalog Card No. 75–1995

0 08 017415 9

SOC
HF
497
B7
1975

BƑ

Robert Manning Strozier Library

JUL 12 1976

Tallahassee, Florida

Printed in Great Britain by A. Wheaton & Co., Exeter

*To the men and women
of many races and divers generations
whose personal story this is.*

CONTENTS

CONTENTS

8

LIST OF ILLUSTRATIONS
AND MAPS

9

J. H. Gaunt, Chairman from 1970

FOREWORD

Having completed 100 years in many and most varied fields of enterprise, the company felt it appropriate to record for those who had taken part—past and present staff—friends and posterity, how we had achieved such success as had come our way, and had taken in our stride what I hope was no more for merchant adventurers than a reasonable proportion of failure.

Mr. Polglase, for many years the highly successful Editor of our *House Magazine*, set himself the considerable task of collecting all available information from which to produce a book: but, as interesting as the bare bones of the story were, they lacked flesh and it was obvious we had to find an author if the story was to have such life as to be of real interest to a wider circle than those who were merely seekers after fact.

Our problem was most happily solved when Mr. Harold Braund was persuaded to accept the task. He had spent himself some thirty-three successful years with the company in Burma, India and Pakistan, and moreover had proved his ability as an author by writing a very readable and successful book about his years of peace and war in Burma. He has not only used Mr. Polglase's valuable material but has collected for himself, much of it during a special visit he paid to this country, as he now resides in Australia. I hope readers will agree that his efforts, and those of the very many who have assisted him from their recollections and their writings at the time, have produced a really fascinating story.

I would emphasise that the intention was to publish a story not a history. Although what has been recorded is to the best of our knowledge factually correct, it was not intended to include everything that might be of importance nor venture to express an opinion as to which Department, which entrepreneur, even which country or period deserved more praise or space; nor, I am sure, can it have done full justice to many who must have contributed much to the happy position in which the company ended its 100th year. To those, therefore, who may rightly feel that their work or experiences justified mention equally, or even more so, than many who have been included, I can only apologise and say that there had to be some limit to the number of people who could be approached and the material used; but there is also our House Magazine, and I am sure the Editor would be delighted to hear from those who can add to the story told in the ensuing pages.

My thanks go to all who assisted in the making or recording of the story, and I hope you will join in conveying our good wishes to those who are already part of the story of what assuredly will be a very different second 100 years. In these years I am sure that Steel Brothers & Company Ltd. will be the same happy, fascinating and exciting company, and that with our excellent staff, and the continuing good friendship of those many individuals and companies with whom we work, we will continue to prosper around the world.

J. H. Gaunt
Chairman,
Steel Brothers & Company Limited.

11

INTRODUCTION

When, in 1945, the dust and the smoke cleared from the world's battlefields, and from ruined cities and ravaged countrysides, nowhere more unashamedly than in the dismemberment of empires was the hand of alliance withdrawn so quickly and the mask of self-interest donned so brazenly.

Imperialism, certainly, had run its course. Henceforward, were it to continue, it could only impose: no longer might it impart. This the Imperial Powers, as a whole, had recognised and accepted; and they were preparing for withdrawal—none more conspicuously than Britain—even before the war. Their remaining commitment was to an orderly bequest, a folding of tents and a stealing away.

It does not fairly lie at Imperialism's door that the process degenerated all too often into a hasty striking of camp, a precipitate leave-taking and a blood bath to fill the vacuum. Those other Powers, *pace* their preachment of 'good government is no substitute for self-government', who ringed the sinking fires and waited for the moment when their financial or ideological dominance could be thrust into the gap created by the disappearance of territorial overlordship, did humanity no service; and millions of nominally liberated people paid with their lives or their happiness.

Many of those whose story follows are of the final generation of Empire; and since this, obviously, must largely be an Asian chronicle, it stands to be asserted that 'colonialism' and 'imperialism' were not the dirty words that fashionably now are preached, and that Steels of the first century may wear their badge with pride.

That the company today perhaps is as prosperous as at any time prior to its unsought divorce from the Far East raises intriguing questions. Certainly for those of Steels' Asian service, after the social upheavals of the First World War, there was little personal enrichment, save perhaps of the spirit. Who can recall a contemporary who left the East with a fortune made and free of the necessity of seeking continuing employment? Did we really exploit the Asian, or did he perhaps, in subtle fashion, exploit us? Who of us took out more than he put in of hard service and affection for the people he lived amongst and worked with? History may yet surprise with its answer.

The task of writing Steels' story has been complicated grievously by the disasters of war. For some seventy years up to 1940, the company's main offices were located in London and Rangoon. In a rapid sequence of holocaust and unholy triumph the one was demolished and the other despoiled. Duplicated records that might have survived had either been spared are beyond the veil. Tales of early years, where living memory is no longer on call, may well smack of romance. Even where memory survives, it can be a frail thing in the minds of old men.

The best possible has been done in this grey area. Many have been consulted: personal records and recollections have been tapped: there has been cross-checking and comparing of notes. As compiler, I have not misunderstood that integrity must infuse the end product; and I have fought shy of the temptation to clothe as fact the occasional hopefully intelligent guess I have permitted myself from the vantage point afforded by holding the ends of so many strings in my hand. If the result sometimes falls short of factual history, I believe it will not be on the grounds of doubtful plausibility.

Once past the grey area, the task has been eased to the point of embarrassment by a surfeit of material available in the pages of the *House Magazine* and the war-time *News Letters*. To successive editors of the former and their many contributors I am extremely grateful. I would single out E. B. J. Polglase, who edited and produced the first number and whose final service, after recurrent periods in the same role, was the assemblage of much of what has come to me as base material for this book. A random dawdling among the pages of the *News Letters* raises a grateful memory of the late Gordon Hundley, who spent six years conjuring them out of the thin air of war-time rationing and censorship for the nourishment of the morale of all. To J. H. Gaunt, an old friend and colleague of pre-war Rangoon days, and now Steels' tenth Chairman, I am grateful for the honour he has done me in entrusting this writing to me, and for his continuing encouragement as the work has moved forward. To J. N. A. Hobbs, at Sondes Place, perhaps I owe sympathy as much as thanks. Dealing with an author at an 'arm's length' of over ten thousand miles must have bred many irritations, but they have not been made apparent. I thank too those others from whom I have had help and advice, particularly the several who have primed me on people, places and projects I have never met or seen. Nor may I omit a word of appreciation of the excellent production of maps that has been undertaken by G. Dinnage of Sondes Place Research Institute. To Wren Publishing Pty. Ltd., of Melbourne, I am grateful for permission to quote and otherwise borrow from *Distinctly I Remember*.

The last but not the least of my acknowledgements is the pleasureable one of recording that a reference to Sir William Strang Steel, at the family seat of Philiphaugh, has brought forth an interested and helpful response. Particularly is Sir William to be thanked for the light he has shed on his grandfather William's commercial history prior to his venture into independent trading, and for the photograph of the Poozoondaung rice mill as it was after its destruction by fire in 1906. Also to be thanked for the 'leg work' he has undertaken in this connection is Ian McGavin, though he would be the first to acknowledge that he has been amply rewarded by the warmth of the hospitality extended to him at Philiphaugh by Sir William and his Lady.

In general terms, I have aimed at a product to be read as literature first and as a public relations exercise second. Some have questioned my recourse to quotations from the writings of others, but, on the broad stage of Steels' story, I feel that there should be some speaking parts at least. In his introduction to *The Men Who Ruled India*, Philip Woodruff described his task as "a rapid survey, while memory lives, of the surface only of the great mass of material that is available". Even at the less ambitious level of Steels' story—I avoid the word "history"—the same cap fits, and I have kept Woodruff's definition before me. I am aware that my selection from all that has come my way will disappoint some. Steels means too many things to too many people for it to be otherwise. Because to me, as to others, is denied the talent to cram a quart into a pint pot, I have aimed rather to inform future curiosity than to bolster past vanity. There has not been room for both. Quoting again from Woodruff—

> To summarize and condense means almost inevitably to be abstract. I have tried instead to be concrete, to take one scene that illustrates a point and to dwell on that, passing mercilessly, though with regret, over many years and places before the next; it is a method less unfair to the reader than abstract comment though still unfair because it selects.

I have introduced the names of individuals as the context, not as distinction, seemed to require. It has been suggested to me that the method is invidious; but I have memories of reading a 'domestic' history, of special interest to me personally, wherefrom the author suppressed all names rather than introduce a few at random. It was bones without flesh. At first mention of names, wherever possible, I have given them in full, with dates of service with Steels in brackets. In one chapter there has been required of me some truncation of colourful events for political reasons. Elsewhere I may risk complaint of a less than up-to-date picture, but I have done my best to observe the year 1970 as the limit of the century. The author of a succeeding volume has his rights.

This introduction would be incomplete without a final tribute. For the greater part of the century traced by the story, Steels operated in lands whence they are now barred or where they survive under some measure of sufferance. There can be no kicking against the pricks. Mankind now orders its affairs differently and 'the moving finger writes and, having writ, moves on'. Few in the more sundered of those countries will have the opportunity to read this story, and those few, probably, will be of generations that are not encouraged to remember.

Let it be proclaimed, nevertheless, that these people belong to the story of Steels as unmistakably as do we who were destined later to follow other trails in other lands, or to retire to the neck of the woods of our own choosing. They were our friends as we sought to be theirs. Much of our *esprit de corps* springs from mutual loyalty and devotion. If we have grown in wisdom it is perhaps because we discovered and absorbed something of the truths they had to offer. Let us remember them gratefully. *Tout passe; l'amitié reste.*

Enough of nostalgia and regret. We are now committed to providing the chronicler of 2070 with his raw material. Since this is unlikely to spring from the teak forest or the paddy field, let us, in our various changes of course, be as Wordsworth's 'Happy Warrior'—

> *Who, with a natural instinct to discern*
> *What knowledge can perform, is diligent to learn.*

H. E. W. Braund
Melbourne, Australia
1974

1870 to 1970

By no still waters did we plough for harvest
  Or idle in the shade of summer's heat:
We found ourselves exotic paths to venture
  On cautious but unhesitating feet.

The crock of gold was seldom where we sought it,
  And rainbows ended over further hills;
Yet treasure is for winning, and we prospered
  In forest, on the oilfields, in the mills.

But turmoil laid a blight on our endeavour,
  We ran a race that was denied an end;
And some there were who perished in the running,
  And fences broke that none are there to mend.

We gathered up the shards of what we fashioned,
  We worked anew with other, stranger clay;
Sought new design, new craftsmen and new cunning,
  And laid to rest the dreams of yesterday.

We march once more in harmony with fortune,
  For time has wrought her miracle of cure:
Here is no tale alone of vanished glory,
  Here is the garb of fresh investiture.

CHAPTER I

THE CENTURY MAKERS

When Queen Victoria's long reign was only half run and William Gladstone was Prime Minister; in the year when Charles Dickens died and the Suez Canal was but newly commissioned; when Paris was under siege and Stanley was setting out on his quest for Livingstone; at a time when the American people were groping for a way of life to replace that which had gone with the Civil War, and the Indian Mutiny was still a nightmare memory for many, a young Scot parted company with his partners in Burma and started trading on his own. The year was 1870; the man was William Strang Steel; his company he launched as W. Strang Steel & Co.

In 1851, Steel, as a young man of nineteen, had been sent to Java as an Assistant in the firm of Martin Dyes & Co. (whose Glasgow principals, Martin Turner & Co., he had joined six years earlier). In 1856 he returned to Glasgow and set up his own business. This, presumably, did not prosper, for in 1857 he went to Rangoon as a Manager for Gladstone Wyllie & Co., a Consignment House. By 1859 he was a partner in this concern, but in 1870 he resigned to found the company whose story is here to be told.

Rangoon, when Steel launched out on his own, was little more than a riverside village, and bamboo predominated as building material. Government House was but a wooden bungalow. Sarkies', the only hotel, was also identifiable as a wooden structure, though little more than a shed in its outlines. Snipe abounded in the swampy surrounds to the future city. Steel traded initially only in the import of piecegoods, but in 1871 he built his first rice mill on the Poozoondaung creek—the opening step in a progress that was to lead Steels to the summit as the largest millers and shippers of rice in the world.

All the more remarkable is it that, in those very early days, a letter to London setting out the specific articles in which the infant company proposed to trade expressly excluded rice as a "dangerous commodity which they would very carefully leave alone". What a somersault is here revealed! Perhaps it is this early evidence of the flexibility that can see yesterday's pitfall as today's opportunity that explains another remarkable reflection. When the Japanese invaders in 1942

17

ended the role of Steels as the only significant survivor of the many companies which for decades had been engaged in the Burma rice milling and shipping trade, a kaleidoscopic diversion was already under way, and had prospered by 1970 on a far wider than the Burmese stage. The year 1942 shook the foundations unbelievably: it did not shatter them.

In 1873 William Strang Steel left Burma to open a London office at No. 6, East India Avenue, in partnership with his elder brother, James Alison Steel. The Burma end of this London house of Steel Brothers & Company, thenceforward carried on by managers in Rangoon, continued as W. Strang Steel & Co. until its assets were transferred to the parent company on the latter's incorporation on 31st December, 1890. William's only recorded return to Burma was in 1881/2 on the occasion of his honeymoon.

When, in the early days of the Second World War, Steels' two principal 'places of business' in London and Rangoon respectively were lost within a few months of each other, the one by bombing, the other by enemy occupation, the historian became a sufferer whose plight is only now apparent. The carbon copy —not to mention its cumbersome predecessor, the product of the copying press* —the original and the duplicate, have always been *sine qua non* to the man of commerce. When both are destroyed the props are gone from under, and much is lost that memory alone was never trusted, nor, alas, indefinitely available to retain.

So it is that there is not much light available to assist a view of the earliest years both East and West. It is thanks to a benign old gentleman, Walter Mill Frames (1882–1934), that a pen picture survives of the original London Office when he joined the company some years before Jack the Ripper started to stalk the gas-lit alleys of the East End. Survivors of Frames' era will best remember him for the copy of *The Pilgrim's Progress* which he presented to every young Assistant leaving for the East for the first time. Frames was still alive and of sound memory when Steels' House Magazine was launched in 1939. Fortunate indeed is it that he was prevailed upon to write of his early days in the company, for it is one of the deepest scoops from the past that is available.

Frames listed the staff of ten from William Strang Steel down to himself and described the original office premises (1873–1887) as comprising two private rooms and a general office. He proceeded—"Juniors started in those days on a salary of £20 per annum, and well can I remember writing on a slip of paper monthly, which was initialled by Mr. Steel before payment, a receipt for One pound, Thirteen shillings and Four pence in letters as well as in figures. One of the duties of a Junior in 1882 was to fetch Mr. Steel cakes and buns from a Bishopsgate Street café when the Chief, as he often did, stayed in the Office for lunch. Other duties were to attend to the fires, copy letters, index books and files, and run errands."

Perhaps the Founder's dedication is more to be admired than his dietary habits!

To Frames also we owe a brief introduction to his Chief's more nebulous brother—"His brother, Mr. James Alison Steel, he used always to address as 'Mr. Steel'. Mr. J. A. Steel took little active part in the business; he signed the

* As seen in Appendix F.

cheques and wrote private letters." Be that as it may, James continued as Vice Chairman until 1893, when he resigned as such through ill health, though retaining a seat on the Board. He never attended another Board Meeting, and the minutes of the Annual General Meeting held on 22nd January 1895 record his recent death.

The contemporaneous Rangoon office lacks any traceable description beyond that in 1902 it was "dismal, dark, cramped and shabby, and pulled down a year or so later to make way for the present building." The "present" building was the older portion, fronting on Merchant Street, of the ultimate suite that extended down Tseekai Maung Tawlay Street—much worthier premises these, though unpretentiously located.

Enough old bungalows survived until the thirties, in the mill area of Rangoon at least, to establish a mental picture of life lived towards the turn of the century in large, gloomy, unpainted, sparsely-furnished edifices—stilt-borne and with hinged, bamboo matting flaps protecting the unglazed windows. They lacked electricity, running water and any but rudimentary sanitary devices. Light would be provided by the hurricane *bhatti* (an invention that in its day must have ranked closely behind the wheel) supplemented by candles. Meals were served from a distant cook-house, umbilically linked to the bungalow by a covered walk-way that served better as a sun shade than as a wind or rain break. In the monsoon, delivery luke-warm to the table of a meal that had been launched piping-hot from the cook-house did not necessarily argue bad staff work. In the hot weather, those able to afford it would hire a *punkah* puller. Here was a remarkable mortal who, from a verandah outside the living rooms, the end of a rope entwined among his toes, would keep one or more long, suspended matting fans idly flapping indoors just above head level, and maintain this for hours on end, apparently even while sleeping. Compensating for the basic drabness were the magnificence of the bougainvillaea rioting over the verandahs and up the walls, and the beds of richly coloured canna breaking the green of the lawns.

Up-country, of course, the primitive would become the barbaric. The Katha Forest manager of 1902 lived in "a ramshackle old bungalow adjoining the native quarter". Visualise, if we can, a hot weather evening on the verandah with an age-old newspaper or a small-print novel falling apart from the ravages of silver-fish or white ants. The open bedroom door provides a glimpse of a *charpoy* shrouded in a heavy netting that effectively thwarts the whisper of a breeze no less than the desire of the mosquitoes. Above our head a silent stream of bats flashes into, along and out of the verandah. A lizard falls with a startling 'plop'. Below the raised floor a group of 'pi' dogs wrangles noisily for the favours of a mangy bitch on heat. Outside it is pouring heavily and relentlessly, and the rain-drops beating on the teak are a constant reminder that it will be as it is now when time comes to venture forth in the morning. There are no kindred spirits to talk to. Another bottle is called for.

The young bachelors in Rangoon were stabled rather than housed in establishments hopefully described as 'chummeries'. On the top floor of the old Rangoon office of living memory was located 'Merry Helenside', the home over many years of the six most junior Assistants stationed in Rangoon at the time. If, by the mothers of nubile daughters at least, it was sometimes regarded as a den of iniquity, it nevertheless moulded and matured some memorable characters in the most positive sense. Old men, in their nostalgic conceit, may be forgiven if they sometimes wonder whether and where such basic training in self-reliance is provided now.

A chronicler of those early days, George Osborne Stiven (1887–1929), tells of a "warm-hearted fellow" who presented a piano to the chummery—"On festive occasions this instrument was not well treated, or maybe was too well 'treated' at times. At last it had to be put to rights and the cost was duly debited to 'Charges general'. When this item was questioned in a letter from London, David, his ire raised, said, 'By ——, the next man who makes any present to the Firm must —— well endow it!' "

Years later another piano was in fact presented to 'Merry Helenside' by the wife of a senior member of the staff, but it 'fell' out of a window one Saturday evening (one suspects an act to thwart the tedium of a two-finger, single-tune practitioner) and, the Merchant Street pavement being two flights down, it was judged to be beyond repair. 'Charges general', therefore, was not invoked.

Stiven's reminiscence continues—"There were several other petty items also questioned by London at that time, including the use of candles for night work, the contention being that cheap oil lamps would cost less! It struck us at the time that the small staff we had then who used candles for working 'overtime' might have been thanked for that rather than any question made!"

Of the people who lived the life of these days, men and women, one is astonished that a light-weight, informal mode of daily wear was so long delayed in coming to the East. It is a matter in which *de rigueur* was all-demanding long beyond the limits of reason. One looks at group photographs of the day, the men hirsute beneath enormous, coal-scuttle *topis*, jacketed and trousered as though for mountaineering; the women heavily draped from head to toe, with only hands and face excluded. One can almost feel the omnipresent prickly heat.

Yet here were people who toiled mightily, learnt the language and earned nick-names coined of affection. They rode horses, not knowing cars; and sweated out their fevers, lacking prophylactics yet undeveloped. They were strangers to the 'wireless' set and the air-mail envelope; they preceded the ice box, let alone the refrigerator. Home leave was infrequent and methods of travel potentially hazardous. The amenities of 1970 would have stunned them by shock, but they belong conspicuously to this story of century makers.

One internal war and three international conflicts cut across this story of Steels. Until 1885 Thayetmyo, on the Irrawaddy, was the nearest British post to the frontier between British Burma and the independent kingdom of Ava to the north. Of the Third Burmese War of 1885–1886, the *Encyclopaedia Britannica*, suitably for present purposes, records the circumstances that led to its being fought and to the conclusion whereby the whole of Burma came under the British Crown—

> The imposition of an impossible fine on the Bombay-Burma Trading Company, coupled with the threat of confiscation of all their rights and property in case of non-payment, led to the British ultimatum of Oct. 22, 1885; and by Nov. 9 a practical refusal of the terms having been received at Rangoon, the occupation of Mandalay and the dethronement of King Thibaw were determined upon.

Both of these objectives were achieved.

The South African, or Boer, War of 1899–1902, coming as it did when the Suez Canal was firmly established as the trade artery between Britain and the Far East, seems to have had little but emotional impact in Burma. A reference to the City columns of the London *Daily Telegraph* of the period yields no light beyond that the London rice market was quiet at the time of the relief of Mafeking. There is no mention of enlistment by members of the London staff. Probably this sort of response to events was not officially canvassed.

The World War of 1914–1918, though it involved no land fighting in the Far East, was a different matter. Here was Britain, with large citizen armies committed to Europe and the Middle East, beleaguered by the German U boat campaign, which laid a stranglehold on all her shipping lanes and exacted tremendous losses of life, tonnage and treasure. Rice cargoes from Burma reached London in ships that were survivors; no longer were they predictable arrivals. The domestic threat to Britain was far more from starvation than from zeppelin-borne bombs.

Of Steels' staff, ninety-two members saw active service beyond the Channel or in India and the Middle East. For twenty of them, nearly all from the London establishment, there was to be no return. They too must be remembered as belonging to this story of century makers.

In the Far East, the impact of war fell most heavily for Steels on the newly ventured oilfields, notably at Lanywa in Burma and Khaur in India, where the development of recent discoveries had almost totally to be deferred. Rice and teak, of course, were among the necessities of war. Both were vigorously harvested and milled, and shipped as opportunity offered. For the Rice Department, indeed, there was an additional upsurge of activity. Pre-war, German millers had been active competitors in Rangoon. On the outbreak, their properties were sequestrated by the Custodian of Enemy Property. Later they were sold and Steels bought those which had been owned by the German-owned Burma Rice and Trading Co. Ltd. Re-styled as the Burma Company Limited, they thereafter became a part of the Steels combine. For the Imports Department, of course, there was little that could be imported.

Though there was no call-up in Burma, the British staff reacted predictably and a number left to join the Forces. In many cases they were commissioned into the Indian Army Reserve of Officers to fill gaps caused by the transfer of regulars to Europe or the Middle East. One at least, James Alexander Liddell (1906–1935) travelled far enough afield that he returned to Steels after the war with a Military Cross (and, incidentally, in the war of 1939–1945, at the age of 60, was back in North Burma as a liaison officer with the U.S. Forces!).

In 1919 many 'recruits' arrived in Burma to fill the gaps caused by the drought of the war years. The inverted commas are a cover to a band of seasoned warriors, several of them decorated and some scarred or lamed. Collectively they represent a generation with whom staff still serving or recently retired have memories of active association—the Managers and Agents of the years between the wars.

Historically the era these men heralded is of importance because it provides the middle distance to this story. It was a period of expansion that saw Steels breaking much new ground. Such was the call for staff in the East that over a quarter of a London establishment of about eighty might be youngsters awaiting passage to Burma or to India, where The Attock Oil Company and the Indian branches of the Indo-Burma Petroleum Company were acquiring significant status.

The London Office, with its Fenchurch Avenue portals and its Lime Street frontage, was self-contained and comprised three floors. Its closely crowding neighbours ensured that it be a gloomy place, and at the time of its death it would have been considered obsolete. To such as Walter Frames, ensconced at the head of the cash desk in carpet slippers (his walking shoes neatly positioned beside the safe), it must have seemed the ultimate in progress. In 1932, fifty years after his initiation, the starting salary was fourfold at £80 per annum; but before embarking on calculation of the rate of inflation indicated by this figure, let there be pause for consideration of a most valuable fringe benefit in the two and sixpenny lunch voucher which junior staff tore out of a perforated book at mid-day or one o'clock according to roster. This guarantee of at least one square meal daily has been widely imitated or varied in later years. It has its origin in a winter's day of 1906, when Mr. (later Sir James) Duncan (1877–1927) returned early from lunch and found, still at their desks, several junior assistants, of whom James Kilgour Michie (1905–1960), a future Chairman, was one. On enquiring why they had not gone out to lunch, he was told that, being the end of the month, they had little or no money left. Mr. Duncan promptly devised and introduced the luncheon-voucher system, which thereafter became a common practice in the City and elsewhere. The vouchers were exchangeable for the equivalent in fare, first at Pimms' then, as a result of some dimly suspected quarrel, at The London Tavern. Both places were later to be destroyed by bombing. A voucher plus threepence to cover a two and ninepenny meal was not unusual: a two and threepenny meal was unheard of and would have been a sacrilegious waste of threepence.

Then there was 'tea money'. In the Rice Department at least, the milling season involved late work on account sales. Labour beyond 6 o'clock carried with it a compensation of one shilling and sixpence an hour. Mostly this was diligently earned; but who would plead not guilty to the occasional evening when, with the clock showing five fifty, some urgent reason for further toil went unfabricated?

Having attained a place on the short list of those destined for early marching orders, Juniors were sent for a few hours a week to the London School of Oriental Languages to start learning Burmese. This preliminary was deemed no impediment to a subsequent posting to India. The managers of those days were heavily Burma-oriented; their Eastern service having pre-dated the 'break-out' into India. To them such places as Rawalpindi savoured of penal settlements. If you found yourself posted there it probably meant, in their eyes, that there was something against you on your confidential file. The tutor of Burmese was a Scot, ex-Indian Civil Service, of whom it was said that no foreigner ever rivalled his mastery of the Burmese language. If in most cases little was learnt, the fault was not his.

A posting overseas was consummated by an act of enormous significance, the signing of a first Agreement for three years (though the normal first *chukka* was five and a half). In a world that has since played fast and loose with currency revaluation, it is impossible now to assess the equivalent of 350 rupees a month

Rangoon office after liberation from the
Japanese—1945

Steels' Senior Rangoon staff—1889

Steels' Rangoon office staff—1937

Top Row—J. G. McCulloch, G. Burns, D. M. Price, J. C. Fraser, J. M. Smith, I. F. Scott, T. R. Arnot, G. H. Hollom.
Next Row—R. C. Scott, J. Pritchard, A. C. S. Dickie, F. R. Turner, J. C. Highet, A. J. Pigou, J. H. Gaunt, G. F. Kinnear, C. Haggarty,
B. T. Williams, G. W. Royds, J. N. C. Killick, R. A. Scoones, C. D. V. Wilson.
3rd Row—D. G. Winters, J. C. Purdie, R. B. Groves, F. D. Edmeades, W. H. A. F. Panton, G. Goodsir, E. G. Hunter, K. Lockley, C. H. Sparshott,
H. W. Grey, A. McGilvray, T. Dunsire, J. N. Carne, H. W. H. Valentine, J. Nicholson, C. F. Shaw-Hamilton, J. G. A. Jeffrey.
Seated—Mrs. Haggarty, Mrs. Wilson, Mrs. Hunter, Mrs. Lockley, J. I. Nelson, Mrs. Hollom, Mrs. Hundley, J. Tait, Mrs. McCreath,
Mr. T. T. McCreath, Mrs. Tait, G. Hundley, Mrs. Kirkwood, G. Howison, Mrs. Nelson, W. R. F. Spearman, Miss McCreath, Mrs. Royds,
Mrs. Nicholson.

Steels' Rugby Football XV—1936

Standing—G. F. Kinnear, I. F. Scott, J. N. C. Killick, D. P. Kenny, G. Burns, A. C. S. Dickie, G. E. Massey, J. G. McCulloch, R. A. Scoones, D. M. Price, R. C. Scott, J. C. Fraser.

Seated—A. J. Pigou, F. R. Turner, J. C. Highet, J. Tait, J. S. Pringle, G. Hundley, D. Lewton-Brain, H. E. W. Braund, L. G. Gaudie. C. F. Shaw-Hamilton, J. H. Gaunt.

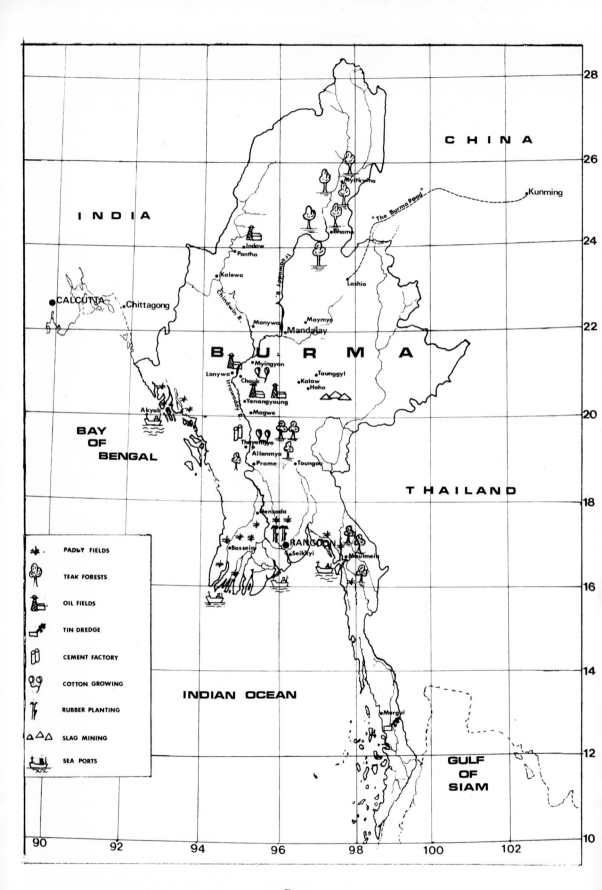

Burma

beyond asserting that it was no stepping stone to affluence. Despatch to Burma normally was by Bibby or Henderson liner, Steels being Rangoon Agents for both.

In Rangoon a stall in 'Merry Helenside' awaited the newcomer and a posse of ex-London friends welcomed him—and the opening of the bar—on board ship. There was a strange sensation to be experienced in seeing these giants of earlier preferment reduced to *chokra* status once more. In circumstances where your bed might be located no more than twenty feet above your desk, the time saved in travel to and from work was consumed in labour; and since all London telegrams had to be decoded by the time the *bo-gyis* arrived at nine, this meant a statutory six o'clock start, with a break for ablutions and breakfast. The lunch 'hour' was a fifteen minute affair taken more or less on the run. Saturdays frequently called for a post-lunch session, and seven to ten on Sundays was the norm, plus, of course, any time consumed in chasing around Rangoon—even unto the distant Mingaladon golf course—with decoded telegrams that appeared to call for instant delivery. Why was it, one wondered, that writers of life in the Far East concentrated so extensively on pink gin, polo and poodle-faking?

Language study now became a deadly striving after social acceptance, for possession of a car or membership of a club alike were denied until minimum requirements had been met. Who could forget those gloomy, desk-bound evenings in the company of a garlic-exhaling *hsaya* whose praise of your progress was as obsequious as it was hollow? Colloquial Urdu presented little difficulty for it is relatively easy to learn, and calls on your proficiency were likely to be limited to announcing your departure for lunch or requesting the conveyance of a note to someone elsewhere in the office. Up-country a knowledge of Urdu was largely irrelevant. Three months sufficed to get you through the exam given a well-disposed examiner. Burmese was a much tougher struggle for it involved learning the written script as well as the spoken word (with its maddening shades of inflexion so necessary to the certainty of knowing whether you were enquiring of a man if his son was at school or in the river). Two years were permitted for success in the Lower Commercial exam. Where talent marched with diligence this time could be halved.

In all this catalogue of sweated labour there was one relieving gleam. Rugby football was never designed for the tropics, but its devotees were not slow to ignore the fact. On sand bank and swamp the game, or some approach to it, has been played in Asia for many years to the bewilderment of local populaces and at the cost of an occasional anti-tetanus injection.

Steels were the only commercial company in Asia with a sufficient headquarters strength to field their own regular fifteen. The fact was a matter of pride at all levels and no objection was likely to be made to the twice weekly getaway from the office. Matches on the Gymkhana Club ground were widely and enthusiastically supported, and the Burma fifteen that went to India every year for the All-India tournament invariably included some Steels representatives.

By the early twenties the bachelor component of Steels' Rangoon staff had far exceeded the accommodation afforded by 'Merry Helenside'. On the 'right side of the tracks' there had arisen the splendour of Kandawgalay House. Re-christening came early, and to generations of the staff it will be remembered as 'The Gin Palace'. The building was a three-storeyed affair with self-contained flats for six single men on each level plus dining and living rooms at ground level. The surrounds were extensive enough for tennis and squash courts and stables. Revelry was frequent, loud and long. One is tempted to speculate that some unruly *nats* are innocuously haunting the place yet.

The senior staff, mostly married, were housed in modern style in such delectable suburbs as Golden Valley. They relied no more on the outside cookhouse, the hurricane *bhatti* or the *punkah* puller. One can recall much in the way of generous hospitality at their hands. It all made for a powerful *esprit de corps*.

However, this dwelling on the fleshpots of the metropolis must not obscure the fact that the sweat of Steels' labours was no more than reflected in Rangoon. From the forests of Myitkyina in the far north to tin dredging leases in the deep south of the Tenasserim archipelago; from the rice mills of Akyab on the west coast to the teak leases on the Siamese border east of Moulmein, Steels' staff were to be found. Their activities covered timber extraction, paddy buying, oil drilling, cotton ginning, cement making, tin dredging and rubber planting. Some of them enjoyed the sparse company and primitive amenities of headquarter stations: others toiled in total or near solitude for months on end in unenviable conditions. There were those who died of blackwater fever or by violent accident, and some who buried wives or children. Some were invalided out, others went by choice on discovering that they had marched to the beat of the wrong drum. A minority, perhaps, look back on a testing education with little of regret and much of gratitude.

At this point we approach the historical explosion that terminated the Burma era of this story of century makers—the third of the major conflicts referred to earlier. It is the appropriate stage of our march, though we risk the obvious charge of prejudice, to attempt the briefest possible appraisal of Steels' impact on Burma. The cynic and the ill-informed would see them as the pawns of Imperialism in the subjection of an ignorant race. How would the jungle Burman view people who, in general, treated him with a consideration that is alien to the oriental temperament? Men who exacted no 'rake off' for his employment but demanded value for what they paid him? Men and women who concerned themselves with the welfare of his family, and frequently with the education of his children if none was otherwise available? If these strange foreigners worked too hard and played too hard and roistered too noisily, what had this to do with the fact that they were to be trusted in a way that their own superiors too frequently were not? If too often they appeared to take the name of their God in vain, at least He seemed to be merciful, long-suffering and of great goodness.

Though we run ahead of the story, let us consider the independent judgment of some post-war reviewers of aspects of the Burma campaign.

Lord Ballantrae, better known to 'Burma hands' as Bernard Fergusson of 'Chindit' fame, writing of the role of the 'boxwallahs', reflects on "the extraordinary loyalty which they inspired in their subordinates from the many races that inhabit Burma. When Britain's sun had dipped far below the horizon and all was dark, hundreds of native employees, some of whom had served the companies for three generations, ranged themselves with their former *Thakins*. They shared their faith and their fate, hiding them, guiding them, and sharing all the risks, because they had learned to trust them. Many of these were killed, and must not be forgotten."

A reviewer in *The Times Literary Supplement* (specifically of guerrilla warfare in the Chin Hills) is unnamed and probably had no personal involvement in the Burma campaign. He conjectures that "the relationship between the Chin soldiers and their British officers must have been profound. In the face of the collapse of British power in Asia after Pearl Harbour they, like several other Burmese hill people, remained loyal to the British when the advantages of disloyalty must have been all too apparent."

Philip Woodruff, in his classic *The Men who Ruled India*, refers to "the Second World War, when the English were in deep adversity and the hill tribes showed them a loyalty as moving as any in history."

If there is some harping on loyalty in the hills, let it be remembered that the hills retained a precarious freedom where Burma of the delta and the river valleys was enemy-occupied. Loyalty must be exercised circumspectly where locally it is likely to be trumpeted as treason. The common thread in the three observations needs little stressing. Why back an Imperialist exploiter when he seems to be on the run?

The holocaust of 1939–1945, if hopefully the war to end war, might well have proved to be the war to end Steels. Its implications for the Company and its staff world-wide were those of total involvement. Nowhere was this more brutally stressed than in the destruction of the London Office in the early hours of Sunday, 11th May, 1941 (by which time, incidentally, over 50 per cent of the London staff of 18 months earlier were on active service). It would be churlish to paraphrase an event such as this when an eye-witness account by a member of the staff is available. J. M. Williams (1939–1941) wrote—

On Saturday evening Liddell, Henderson and I, as members of the Fire Fighting Squad, were sitting around the small electric fire in the basement just in the usual way expecting the siren to go as the R.A.F. bombers had visited Berlin the previous night. Rightly enough the wireless went off the air and soon after we heard the alert. I immediately put on my steel helmet and took my axe and gas mask.

I then went up on to the roof and asked Liddell to help me carry up additional buckets of sand, water, scoops and a stirrup pump. After this we remained on the roof and watched incendiaries which had been dropped on nearby roofs, burning with a bright white glare. The drone of enemy aircraft could be heard overhead and occasionally the explosion of H.E.s (high exposive bombs) in the near distance. As I was descending the ladder leading from the roof of Mrs Young's apartment I heard the whistle of 3 or 4 H.E.s dropping very close and, one actually hitting the building, there was a flash, an explosion and I felt 'No. 6' shudder beneath me as I slid down the remaining rungs of the ladder.

After Liddell had joined me we went down the stairs where the atmosphere was thick with dust which prevented us from seeing or even breathing properly. I switched on my torch, the light from which scarcely penetrated the 'fog' and soon I had to put on my gas mask which proved a great help. Walking over broken glass and fallen doors we eventually reached the Timber Department where we met Fire-watchers from next door. One of them noticed a fire starting in the department and walking along the edge of the hole caused by the H.E. we extinguished the fire with two buckets of water. We continued on down the stairs and noted that the bomb had finally exploded in the Rice Department, where it appeared to have caused extensive damage; the cap of the bomb had fallen through into the Equipment Room close to my bed and was soon removed.

After this incident everybody went to the lower shelter where we settled down, some of us on chairs and others lying on mattresses. Fortunately there had been no casualties.

From then on we went up at intervals to make certain the building was safe from fire. At approximately 3.45 a.m. the next door Fire Party leader came in again and mentioned that, although the worst part of the raid was over, we should still keep watch in case the roof was set alight by flying sparks from adjacent fires.

I put down my book and quickly went up the stairs on to the roof and no sooner had I arrived on the roof than I heard the whistle of an H.E. followed by a terrific explosion. This time I was quite prepared to see the whole building collapse under me. Fortunately the roof of 'No. 6' stood up to it once more and as soon as it was over I started going down the stairs by the light of my torch and again had to wear my gas mask. When I got to the Oil Department I could go no further as the remaining part of the staircase had collapsed.

For a while I felt rather desperate and actually shouted for help but, as nobody answered, I realised I had to act on my own. I could see flames and smoke coming up from below but paid little attention to this as I hurried back onto the roof with the idea of crossing to the adjoining building by way of the connecting wooden bridge. Having got there I went down to their basement, thence into ours where I witnessed a most distressing and pitiable scene. Out of the nine people in the shelter all but one had been more or less seriously injured.

By the time the blackened shell of the building had been demolished, Mrs Young, the long-time housekeeper, had died with her charge, as had four of her companions in the basement shelter.

So passed No. 6, Fenchurch Avenue, after a contribution of 54 years to this story of century makers.

In Burma on the day of destiny, the 3rd September 1939, in chummery and logging camp, men sat around their radio sets, glass in hand—for it was that time of day with them—and listened to Sir Neville Chamberlain telling the British people that they were at war with Germany—for the second time in the memory of older listeners.

Reactions must have been many and varied, spontaneous and pondered; but letters of resignation coupled with requests for earliest possible passage westward were a common response. However, all such were blocked by a Government order to all firms that resignations were not to be accepted without the approval of Burma Command, who clearly were not prepared to countenance the draining of a pool of Burmese-speaking potential officer material. Events were to prove them right.

So, through the period of the 'phony' war, business proceeded outwardly as usual. With the defeat of France, however, the pattern changed and Steels' Assistants, among others, progressively found themselves under orders to report at Maymyo for training for full-time military service. Naturally enough, the least indispensable, the juniormost, were the first to go. The end result tended towards a reversal in uniform of civilian seniority for those older men whose release to the forces was longest postponed. For an aggrieved minority, of course, there was no release at all. Someone had to keep the wheels turning, even though it be with one pair of hands where three had been needed before.

With the entry of Japan into the war, familiar figures disappeared into the blue as company commanders of Burma Rifles or Burma Frontier Force units, or put to sea as officers in coastal patrol ships of the Burma Navy. One, though early to be killed in training, joined the Burma Air Force, which then was starting from scratch.

It is not within the acceptable limits of this story to catalogue individual war records and achievements. They were many and varied, for the Burmese-speaking ex-civilian with jungle experience was a god-send to newly-arrived regular units for whom too much was bewilderment in a terrain for which neither training nor previous fighting had prepared them. Mercifully a significant number of regular commanders of active formations were quick to welcome a junior lieutenant, knowing little of military formality, who, on a still moonlit night, could explain with confidence the 'tonk tonk' of the coppersmith bird or the cry of a barking deer; and could establish a working relationship with local Burmans who spoke no English.

The limit will be set by sampling, through other than Steels' eyes, from the aggregate contribution made by Steels' staff to the Far Eastern war effort—

J. K. Stanford (Indian Civil Service) writing of R. E. Hall (the first recorded British casualty in the Burma fighting)—

> Poor Raymond! the last of the dandies and not the least well-loved, the best of company, a *viveur* and a lover of ponies who in his remote jungles, for nine months in the year, worshipped his polo boots, which he kept in a sort of flannel cradle like twin babies and fed on cream. Raymond whom the gods loved as well as men, who never guessed on that eventful night of rejoicing that he would one day meet a lonely end at the hands of the Japanese.

Bernard Fergusson writing of J. C. Fraser—

> I read a report, in an Intelligence Summary some weeks later, of John Fraser's capture, escape and appalling journey of 54 days, in the course of which two of his companions were drowned, and he himself rescued from drowning by the skin of his teeth. I read and marvelled at his story; but never thought that he and I were to be so closely associated in the near future, and to owe each other our two lives.

Ian Morrison (War Correspondent of *The London Times*) writing of Arthur Thompson (now the well-known author, Francis Clifford) and Noel Boyt—

> The company, about 150 strong, was under the command of Captain A. L. B. Thompson, formerly of Steel Brothers, and held a strong Japanese vanguard for several hours at the twenty-eighth milestone, inflicting heavy casualties. Boyt, by dint of driving all night from Mawchi, arrived in time for the battle and both he and Thompson had narrow escapes, Boyt being blown up (but only slightly injured) by a mortar bomb and Thompson having a dud bomb roll down the hill between his legs. When it became clear that they were greatly outnumbered and could no longer hold the Japanese, they withdrew up the road blowing all the bridges. This action, for which Thompson was later awarded the D.S.O. and Boyt the M.C., and the destruction of the bridges, delayed the Japanese for several days and gave the Chinese 6th Army time to prepare positions east and west of Mawchi where they fought stubbornly.

Presidential citation accompanying the award to P. E. Quinn of the Legion of Merit, the U.S.A.'s highest decoration for distinguished and meritorious service by non-Americans—

> Captain Patrick E. Quinn, Indian Army, displayed exceptionally meritorious conduct in the performance of outstanding services with the Office of Strategic Services in North Burma from October 1942 to April 1945, engaging almost continually in intelligence operations far behind the Japanese lines. In spite of the ever-present danger of capture, made more acute by the fact that he operated without the security offered by a large body of men, he used natives to set up road checks and intelligence screens which secured highly valuable information of terrain and aerial supply. Captain Quinn led his group in a manner which inspired their confidence and contributed materially to the success of the Allied forces from Fort Hertz to Lashio.

Others there were whose comparable exploits went unhonoured and unsung. Others yet did not survive; and here must be remembered those who in civilian garb—older men most of them—exhausted themselves in the cause of 'scorched earth' and then faced jungle paths leading to an India too far distant for their remaining strength and spirit to take them. One is buried in a rest house garden; at least one other beside the bullock cart track where he dropped. Let them be commended, as century makers, to the assurance of the writer of Ecclesiasticus— "And some there be which have no memorial—but their name liveth for evermore."

We have referred to the members of Steels' staff in Burma to whom military service was denied on the grounds of age or impracticability. Let extracts from the writings of two of them illustrate how nebulous was the distinction between military uniform and civilian garb when the end came.

Joseph Boardman Clark (1923–1958) wrote—

Let me try and briefly describe the scene at the Rangoon docks on the morning I left by my firm's river convoy with 6000 employees on the first stage to Mandalay.

A column of depressed-looking Indian soldiers was being formed up on the quay as they stepped off a trooper, whilst thousands of hysterical people were surging towards the dock gates in full panic, clamouring loudly for sea passages. Looters were busy in the deserted shops and houses, and an occasional exchange of shots or the firing of a store served to add to the general pandemonium, to the accompaniment of the shrieks and antics of lunatics released that morning from the asylum. The wail of the air-raid siren completed the confusion, but mercifully there were no bombs.

No time was lost in getting as many refugees on board the few available ships as they could hold, but many were left behind to find their way out by the land routes or stay and take their chance with famine, fire or disease.

Before these ships could return from the short trip to India, for more evacuees, the docks were a mass of smoke and flame, the Rangoon river itself was afire after the refineries had been scorched, and the Japanese had arrived with yet another New Order.

Two months later, at the end of April, came the turn of Mandalay which, on the morning I last saw it, was literally razed to the ground except for the old fort. . . .

No signs of evacuees here, except corpses, for the living had all moved on, and if they had food with them for a three or four weeks' trek, then they had a chance, provided they could reach the Chindwin before the advancing Japs.

. . . The railway station a hollow shell, the lines littered with a twisted mass of mangled metal, smouldering coaches and the bare ribs of engines lying on their sides. This was Mandalay on 23rd April 1942, when we set out for the last stage of our retreat from Burma.

Over 5800 of my original party of 6000 had already been escorted into India, and we were now left with 136 Indians, mostly barge and launch crews who had remained behind to ferry petrol for the R.A.F., for whose return two of us had promised to wait. In addition there were three of the best Burmese clerks I ever had, who elected to come out with me and are now helping the Army in the Return to Burma.

The stage by river to Katha was easy, for we had plenty of food and stores on board our launch, the *Wigaro*, on which I had lived since 25th February.

In fact, we quite enjoyed this stage of our retreat and it was with a feeling of sadness that I took my last glimpse of the top deck of the *Wigaro* as she settled down on the river bed at Katha, until only 6 inches of funnel was visible. 50 or 60 other launches lay with her.

I kept the compass and the ship's bell—so she came with us on our trek to India and the compass proved invaluable.

Our course from Katha lay via Banmouk to the Chindwin, which we crossed at Homalin a day before the Japanese arrived. Then over the forbidding Naga hills to Manipur one week behind General Stilwell and his party.

It looks a short hop on the map from Katha to Imphal, but it is actually a little over 500 kms. For the first stage of 100 kms from Katha to Mansi, just beyond

Banmouk, we travelled by lorry and bullock cart, the next 150 kms was by bamboo rafts to Homalin. The last 250 kms we travelled on foot.

Our knowledge of the language and the fact that we had silver coins with us helped to obtain the services of coolies and guides from the hill tribes, which lightened the loads we each had to hump and enabled the weaker members of the party to be carried at times when they became exhausted.

On the way we picked up seven walking Tommies whose rations were exhausted. We also took in train some tired and exhausted Indian soldiers, five or six women and a little Gurkha boy of 5 who walked the whole distance unaided and seemed to like it.

Just as in the previous stages of our retreat from Burma, we received kindness, hospitality and assistance from the remaining Burmese at every place we passed.

The second account comes from the pen of Percy George Graham Salkeld (1915–1968), Steels' Deputy General Manager at the time—

On the morning of 10th May the party, then consisting of thirty-seven persons, fourteen being British, including ten Steels men, left Maingkwan with a number of elephants (from Steels' forests), also some bullock carts, and proceeded by a diversion from the normal route to the first big stream we had to cross, one of the headwaters of the Chindwin, and for the whole of this stage of six miles we were drenched with rain. We arrived at the river, unloaded the bullock carts, paid the cartmen off because they could proceed no further, and then loaded up the kit on the elephants before sending them across the river. We crossed in boats manned by local Kachins, who were splendid fellows . . . and then proceeded on a ten-mile march through dense jungle, being much annoyed by leeches and the same for the next two days . . . after three days' marching we arrived at the Turunghka river, which appeared deep and was being crossed by ferries carrying large numbers of refugees, but we decided to cross the party on the backs of our elephants—up to which event we had made it a rule that only the sick were allowed to ride elephants on the march. . . . Then we made our way by no more than a mule track to Shinbwiyang, passing the remains of many people and animals, the former having died from exhaustion or cholera. . . .

At Shinbwiyang we stayed a full day to rest, dry out the kit and get organised for what was now to be the real hard going, as henceforth there were few villages, few clearings for planes to drop rations and most of the country was little known. In addition, food for the rest of the journey until we could get in touch with help from the Indian side had to be carried. Here also we had to try and persuade some of our elephant men, all Burmese, to come on into India, and eventually eleven of them agreed to come with us. . . . With our transport so assured, we set out next morning in fine weather and made good progress.

We were away to an early start—it was a gruelling march, and a steady uphill path climbing to 4800 feet, passing more corpses. The mud was pretty grim at times, pockets being knee deep, and understandably this form of walking was very exacting for most of us, who were pretty tired before we ever set out on the walk, and most of us were suffering from tummy trouble, no doubt brought on by poor food and cooking, damp and exhaustion, though on the other hand the majority of us in ourselves felt reasonably fit. On the second day, after crossing the Namyang, we came across two Europeans lying by the side of the path in a bamboo hovel, both completely exhausted and from first appearance on the point of death. One was a sergeant of a famous British regiment who had had cholera, and though he had got over this, was too weak to move and had been lying there for six days with practically nothing to eat; the other was a lad out of the Rangoon Customs who had been lying there for four days with a high fever—malaria, and also had had practically nothing to eat. . . . We fixed them up with a blanket each and gave them some warm Horlicks, of which we still had a small bottle, a little brandy (from a flask which I was guarding very closely against such emergencies), and told them we would carry them with us next day, which revived them a lot. . . . Two days after this the advance members of our party came across the first signs of help from India. . . . Next day we had a very trying march—consisting of seven miles uphill and about six down—but the distance seemed twice as far and it took some of us, with a certain amount of very strenuous bamboo-cutting, to clear a way for our elephants and the large carrier baskets strapped to their backs, from 8 a.m. to 6 p.m.—the going at this point was dreadful, corpses still being fairly frequent. At the end of the march, however, we received a wonderful welcome from two tea planters and a young British police officer who gave us strong, hot tea, drunk out of discarded bully-beef tins, which we were grateful to get, and an army biscuit each, which was as good as the best cake as we had been without biscuits ever since Shinbwiyang. We were also presented with two tins of Australian 'Camp Pie', very good. . . . During this night, 26th May, our sergeant patient died and after his burial we resumed our march. . . .

The discipline of our party can best be gauged by the fact that no one went for more than one day without a shave—a good show. . . . It was a march more good for the soul than the body, and as I remarked on one or two occasions to cheer the party up, when trying to camp for the night in the rain—'good practice for worse'(!!). I sincerely trust, however, that should it be my lot someday to return to Burma, I do not have to walk back in the rain via the Hukawng Valley.

As an exemplar of a commercial company whose staff members, in conditions of unimaginable disaster, consistently had displayed the highest standard of self-lessness, courage and efficiency in saving what they did from a frightful spate of human misery, John Tait, Steels' General Manager in Burma, was knighted. It was a recognition that entitled many men and women to wear its reflected glory.

The honours won by Steels' staff in, or in close association with, the Armed Forces on all fronts in this war of 1939–1945 speak for themselves—

Distinguished Service Order	1
Officer, Order of the British Empire	1
Member, Order of the British Empire	5
Distinguished Service Cross	1
Military Cross	9
Military Medal	1
Mentioned in Despatches	47

The 'mentions' were won by women as well as men, by civilians as well as military; and they were conferred on British, Anglo-Burmans, an American and an Indian. However, on the other side of the medal were the names of seventeen century makers for whom victory was a known or an unmarked grave. They died in England, Europe, North Africa, the Middle East, India and Burma. It was a very heavy price.

During their exile from Burma, Steels established their headquarters in the Indo-Burma Petroleum Company's offices in Calcutta. Not the least of the services they rendered here—and one wonders how 'security' was not sometimes breached—was the relaying Home of news of staff on active service, news which then would be phoned by the London Office to wives or parents who otherwise might have heard nothing for weeks or months. The morale content of this sort of thing is immeasurable.

In a more official way, the accent was heavy on planning for the Return that none doubted must come. However, the war was far from over and, in 1943, its prosecution was tragically aggravated by an appalling famine in Bengal—right on the frontier of battle. The Indian Tea Association, with their gardens in the affected area, were forced by necessity to co-ordinate the procurement and distribution of rice for their large staffs in a single, central scheme in order to eliminate any tendency to compete for the limited supplies available. Steels, with temporarily frustrated expertise available, were called in to help, and found themselves playing a role that improbably was to last for 25 years until 1968, at which time foreign firms in India were debarred from accepting agency commitments of any kind, and the contract passed into the hands of a locally incorporated company.

The surrender of Japan and the liberation of Burma found Steels planned and poised for an extremely costly programme of rehabilitation in which, regrettably, His Majesty's Government in the United Kingdom proved reluctant to play more than a token part, despite the denial by destruction committed in its name three years earlier. Sadly, however, and this was the more important, concurrent winds of change were blowing from Burma itself; winds by which many simple people were not to benefit. Burma's fortunes now lay in the hands of ardent nationalists, many of whom had aided and abetted the Japanese during the period of their occupation. They were able to capitalize, of course, on the manifest demonstration that the bubble of British invincibility had been pricked—and by an Asian people at that. Though there was prompt acceptance of Steels' restorative and conciliatory genius, nationalization followed in depressing sequence as working conditions were re-established. In retrospect, however, it was a cynical hoax that Steels, and the other Burma companies with them, should earlier have recognised as such. Be that as it may, it is all now a matter of history; and 25 years later Steels enjoy a measure of prosperity that is denied to the Burmese people at large, surrounded as they are by natural wealth that is largely rotting on the vine.

J. K. Stanford, previously quoted, was a prolific and perceptive writer on the subject of Burma, and he was known to many of Steels'. If, for an epitaph, we borrow from him, the bitterness of his reflecting will no more than be in the mood of a basically sunshine story that ended in tears—

> But, it does no good remembering such things now! We have declared, and the side making the runs at present uses jeeps and Sten-guns and 'democratically elected majorities' to enforce their rule, and we were only capitalists exploiting the country during our innings for our own unworthy ends. But . . . I think we were lucky enough to know the old Burma, and to know, too, the jungle Burman as he was before he really knew himself, a man of courtesy and humour and great simplicity, who was 'passing rich' on twenty pounds a year. He lived what seems now an enviably untrammelled and archaic life, five hundred years behind the times, and had never heard of 'Demahkerazi', which, as Kipling's Sudanese put it, is 'a devil inhabiting crowds and assemblies'. And now Fate has jumped on him and given him what he calls 'Home Yew', and he has to be not a simple *taungthu* any more but a Communist, or a *galone*, or an Anti-Fascist People's Freeman, or whatever label his politically-minded masters devise for him.

Let there be no forgetting, however, the tens of thousands of Burmese men and women who belong to this story of century makers. They were wonderful people to live and work with. They are unlikely to play any part in the second century of Steels. This story does not exaggerate their dominance of the first.

For Steels' staff, as the gates to Burma closed, there were sad and drastic partings of the ways; and the dismemberment of closely-knit teams of experts in many fields. For some the years of military service had set up a barrier of no return, and they left to seek their fortunes elsewhere (though remarkable it is how many of them are still to be seen at Company reunions of one sort or another).

For others there was transfer to strange places in distant lands, where they came to terms with their exile or lived with their memories according to individual fashion.

For those of the Burma oilfields and refinery there was a path to something approaching familiar ground. In the North-West of India (soon to become Pakistan) the fortunes of The Attock Oil Company, launched by Steels in 1913, had prospered under conditions where the Government of India had subsidized the search for new oil as a matter of war-time urgency. The dispossessed Burma staff were the answer to an immediate problem. For a rump of the Rice Department there were the years of procurement for the tea gardens of Bengal and Assam already referred to. Within Burma itself, high hopes spurred a return to the traditional buying and shipping of rice. None could offer better credentials, but not for long was there to be more than the pretence of welcome. For the Forest Department there were brave attempts at re-establishment in the forests of Tanganyika and British Guiana, but natural limitation in the one case and political considerations in the other set a limit of a few years to both ventures.

The Indo-Burma Petroleum Company, shorn of its Burma oilfields, its tanker *Shwedagon* and the authority that goes with the command of your own source of supply, nevertheless survived vigorously within the complex of the all-Companies marketing arrangements in India until nationalistic pressures influenced the sale to Indian interests in 1970 of a company that had been initiated by an Indian. In Rangoon, the Imports Department flourished for some years after the war; but, for depressingly familiar reasons, it too died the contemporary death. Elsewhere in Burma, the Cement Company at Thayetmyo was re-activated but then nationalized. In Tenasserim the tin dredge, having been wrecked beyond the limits of resurrection, as dictated by lack of finance and absence of security, was sold for scrap. The tale could proceed, but only as a tedious repetition of events. In other chapters will be found some expansion of these briefly recorded events.

In London, the Export Department, no longer in the role of provider to oilfields, mines, mills and the like, shrank to a shadow of its former self, though the post-war years were to see a compensatory replacement by a growing and successful diversion into the competitive fields of insurance, property development, secondary industry and other activities.

In the Middle East, a close association with the old-established firm of Spinneys, wholesalers and retailers in distributive trades, with special departments operating in the imaginative fields of contract catering and supermarkets, has signally prospered to mutual advantage. Though the nationalistic bitterness that pervades the area has produced its rude shocks, it has also spurred expansion. In East Africa, a comparable association with A. Baumann & Company, themselves already established among the newly independent countries of that region, has prospered to the extent permitted by change to indigenous governmental control.

More than anything else, perhaps, has Steels' expansion first into Canada and then into Australia demonstrated that, having grown up international, the Company sees its future assured by staying that way. With the imagination that launched such diversions there was, maybe, a salting of impertinence; for here are not peoples requiring training in the running of their own affairs. Still less is there scope for sending British youngsters to the London School of Oriental Languages to learn 'Strine' and then posting them to Melbourne. There is a stark difference between the native Canadian or Australian and the jungle Burman, no matter how much each might benefit by knowing the other. No, the intrusion into these lands has been by association of surplus funds and energy with local talent lacking only a wider stage. It could prove a good basis for marriage.

The historian, in 2070, of the second century of Steels, will face a task so different from that of the present writer as to defy imagination or prediction. If, hopefully, he lives in a world that has triumphed over the problems of pollution and human survival by the rejection of nationalistic self-seeking, then he should have much to tell.

CHAPTER II

RICE

Nude to the waist, clad in tattered clothings to the knees, and canopied under a wide, mushroom-shaped *topee* plods he—a stolid child of Nature. His left hand urging the tail of a time-battered plough and his right hand brandishing a muddy rattan, he drives a team of forbearing oxen. The good earth beneath him splits and breaks. Big drops of rain fall with a thud on his huge *topee* and trickle silently on the furrows below. The blowing wind hurls molecules of water at his face and half-exposed body. They hurt him not. Neither chill his ardour. As drenched, he receives them, with wonted stoicism, nay welcomes them amidst wreaths of smoke that make a hasty passage from his sturdy bamboo pipe.

The dreary day struggles on broken only by a simple meal of rice and *ngapi*. Night comes. The day's work is over. The unkempt figure trudges his way home—weary man. Another simple meal of rice and *ngapi*. A puff or two at the narcotic pipe. A cup or two of plain tea, boiling hot, 'the cup that cheers but does not inebriate'. Drowsiness creeps over him. Fatigue overcomes him and soon he is buried in deep sound sleep.

Thus picturesquely has 'Beeloogyun' sketched for us, in Steels' House Magazine, the first link in the long chain that leads from the paddy field to the rice pudding; a peasant, remembered as friend and philosopher, who is unlikely to find any place in the story of Steels' second century.

Herein is sadness, for, by any reckoning, the Rice Department carried the pennant as Steels' senior service—even unto the day when juniors, with their bonuses cut, grumbled at a hierarchy that persisted, in the name of tradition, in ploughing what had become a doubtfully profitable trading furrow.

History must be invoked to provide perspective, and there can be no improving on an account written by J. B. Clark some thirty years ago—

The dawn of the 19th Century found the Burmese Empire passing through an era of uncertainty. For years the country had been engaged in war, at first with success and latterly with the tide of fortune somewhat against her, and the urgent preoccupations accompanying such a state of affairs naturally caused contacts with the outside world to be of a very scanty and unimportant nature. Trade was consequently almost non-existent, and the country's enormous potential resources remained almost entirely unexplored.

The historians have it that the tendency of the rulers in those days was to discourage rather than do anything to foster the development of trade. The arbitrary means of government is said to have made it almost a peril for an individual to become distinguished through wealth—means were always at hand to confiscate that wealth should it become known—and the effect of such circumstances upon any sources of internal trade and those who might have been willing to work and develop them can be readily imagined.

In these early days rice, in the crude form in which it was produced, was already the most abundant product of this land, but export to foreign countries was totally prohibited, as it was feared by the King and Court of Ava that once the peasantry of Lower Burma had reaped the benefit of selling surplus supplies to India, where British trade connections were already becoming well established, or to the Straits, and succeeded in obtaining world values for their produce, it would be difficult to prevail upon them to reserve sufficient stocks for the needs of Upper Burma. The trade, if trade it may be called, was restricted to the transport by small coastal sailing vessels, making but a single trip each season, of such rice as they were able to lay their hands on in the south for the granaries of Upper Burma, which in those days included Assam and Arakan.

The vast Delta, which today covers an area of ten million acres of fertile paddy land, remained an undeveloped swamp and the sailing ships from the rapidly growing rice-importing countries of the world bound for India, Siam and Indo-China passed Burma by and knew her not. For many years Burma, later to become the largest rice-exporting country in the world, continued to sleep.

In 1852, amidst a growing inclination on the part of the leaders to heed the counsels of the few British traders in the country, the second Burmese War came to an end and in 1853 relations between King Mindon and the British had so improved that the latter withdrew their blockade of the river, a declaration of peace was issued and the way was then opened fully for the traders to get down to the business of trading. . . .

Development during the early years was slow, but gradually the news that Burma had a surplus crop of rice available for export came to the ears of millers in the United Kingdom, who found their usual sources of supply from Carolina stopped by the American Civil War and the liberation of slaves. . . .

The settled conditions born of British rule soon provided tremendous impetus to the cultivation of paddy, and British ships provided the facilities for transport. Then came the opening of the Suez Canal in November 1869 and, with the first passage of steamers loaded with cargoes of rice through the canal in 1872, the Burma trade went from strength to strength. . . .

Almost the whole vast area of ten million acres in Lower Burma, as distinct from Upper Burma, has been brought under cultivation during the past seventy-five years—the period which coincides with the rapid growth of Steel Brothers from small beginnings to the pre-eminent position occupied today as the largest millers and shippers in the rice trade of the world.

It needs to be added that the vast expansion described took place in a countryside thinly populated and without resources. The factors above all that wrought the transformation were the recruitment of many thousands of labourers from South India and the injection of Indian capital on a large scale. That this was to create sociological problems for the future does not detract from the magnitude of India's contribution to the foundation of Burma's pre-Second World War self-sufficiency. Even in retrospect it is hard to see how else it could have been achieved in a world that was gaining speed.

In the early days, of course, it was the rising tide of paddy that went westward to the established mills in the United Kingdom. Soon, however, under economic incentive and as later to be described, the mills began moving eastward to the paddy. Whichever it was, the cultivator in the delta had still to face the problems that assailed him when it came to moving his harvest from the threshing floor to the port.

'Beeloogyun' continued his story of the 'stolid child of Nature' by painting in the relaxed, laughter and hope-filled days that lay between seed-time and harvest.

Then came the day when a mound of golden grain stood on the beaten earth in front of his house. And then? Then came the money lenders, the landlord and the brokers with their warnings of falling markets.

Fortunately for the cultivator, a time was to come when the buying of his produce would be shifted from the mill to the threshing floor; but let us first look at a scene described by James McCracken (1905–1954) of the proceedings at Steels' old Lower Kanoungtoe mill, whither he was posted as 'number two' in 1906—

Negotiations started with the appearance of brokers' runners, who advised the expected arrival of the fleet at Kemmendine. There was tremendous competition between runners to get the news in first. Invariably the runners . . . hadn't a ghost of a chance of influencing any of the boats to the mill, but that did not matter. The coming of the *loungzats* was an event that all desired to be associated with.

The next stage was the actual arrival of the fleet. In the first instance they moored on the riverside at Kemmendine. To witness their arrival on a moonlit night was an unforgettably beautiful sight, all rowers putting their backs into it, chanting their river song the while. Sails were spread if a suitable wind prevailed. Everything was done with a little bit of extra swank to mark the end of the voyage.

Safely moored, the real fun began. Brokers and runners by the dozen pestered the traders and boatmen unceasingly. Tall tales they told of the generosity of their respective Godown Masters, but whatever the tale all of the traders eventually visited Steels. . . .

The morning was the time for the first visit. A launch-load of traders, usually headed by Ko Chan Aye, our Kemmendine broker, arrived with the visiting *burra sahib* and on the latter's departure the first rounds of the battle commenced, generally in the nature of a verbal sparring match. The health of our mutual friends, the great misfortunes experienced in the harvest (this a hardy annual!), the remarkably high prices that had had to be paid in order to secure this, the finest shipment from the riverside this year—and so on, filled in a good part of the morning.

Next followed orations on the amazing prices obtainable at all other mills. Then a few requests. So many tins of Rangoon well water would be required for each boat, also a bag of rice per boat for food. Safe space on the mill bank for tying up might also be a stipulation.

Late in the evening a tired and sleepy conference would break up, to be resumed the following morning. In the meantime the violent attacks by competitors had increased, and with the knowledge that Steels had won the first round one or two of the weaker traders would be enticed at great expense to go elsewhere.

After a further day's talk—all very good fun as a rule—the first of the boats would pull up to the mill. This was considered a great victory. . . . The contented boatmen at our mill—and we saw they were contented—soon gathered in the greater part of the other boats. We always lost a few to competitors, but that was expected. Some of the crews were very tough and we had some good scraps at times, but on the whole they were a cheery crowd.

These big boats worked slowly. Built on graceful lines at a high cost, the carving on some of them was as fine as could be seen throughout the country. The owners and boatmen were fully conscious of the picture their boats made, particularly when under full sail. . . . A trip a month for six months of the year was as much as the 'big boats' did.

In its origins and for many years, this was the pattern of rice trading in Burma. Such colourful days were to depart, however, for after the First World War influences for change were at work. Firstly, reaching zenith by about 1923, a proliferation of small mills, some with a capacity of no more than ten tons of paddy a day, began to spread out from the port along the lines of communication in the delta. Some of these were owned by well-to-do locals keen to become rice millers. Some represented tactical transfers aimed at milling for local consumption at more remunerative rates. Some were influenced by the need to ensure first pick of the paddy crop for, increasingly, the overseas demand for rice was laying stress on quality.

Of greater moment yet was the world-wide financial crisis of 1929. Even before this an erosion of integrity had been creeping into the dealings between broker and cultivator in the delta. The more reputable of the brokers had been steadily retiring under the strain of the intrusion of the less scrupulous, who were prepared to adulterate their purchases with inferior grain or otherwise debase their role. When the crash came most of the survivors of the old guard collapsed and defaulted. It then became difficult, in this rice bowl of the world, to keep the Rangoon mills supplied with good-quality paddy in sufficient quantity. Obviously a new approach to the movement of the crop from the threshing floor to the mill had to be sought, and a fair deal for the cultivator was where it had to start.

So it was, in 1930, that the first essay into what became known, and widely practised, as Jungle Buying was launched by the establishment of a Steels' headquarters on the Irrawaddy near Henzada. This was followed in the next few years by many other similar jungle buying stations in the Irrawaddy delta. By 1936 similar establishments were operating to serve the mills at the ports of Bassein and Moulmein.

The reaction of the new order of brokers, threatened by this intrusion into a preserve regarded strictly as theirs, was predictable. They did all in their power to thwart the effort. They started a severe price war and launched a propaganda campaign in the jungle villages. They put it about that the Europeans had come to rob the cultivator of what little profit remained after he had paid his rent and his taxes. Paddy owners were urged to sell only to buyers they already knew, and their natural distrust of strangers prompted them to accept such advice initially. The campaign did not last long. Whispers of fair dealing at the hands of 'Sa-tee' (Steels) started to circulate, and it was not long before suspicion died at the feet of the friendly relationships that were established between the jungle buying staff and the many, great and small, with whom they came to have dealings.

'Jungle Buying', indeed, heralded a revolution. Under the old system a trader used to bring his gig and crew to 'his' part of the delta, buy and load his cargo at possibly two or three villages and then despatch it to his broker at the mill. This leisurely procedure delayed news of purchase and despatch of paddy sufficiently to present the broker with an opportunity of gambling on the market (wherein the price of failure was liable to be passed up the line).

Steels' jungle buying Assistants were provided with speedboats, built by The British Power Boat Co. Ltd. (Rangoon Agents—Steel Brothers & Co. Ltd.), capable of speeds up to 30 miles per hour. This made possible the buying of paddy over a wide area during the course of a single day. Steel-hulled power barges capable of carrying 120 tons of paddy, twice the capacity of the gigs and much faster, were soon supplementing the latter.

The gigs were to a great extent built and maintained at one of Steels' Rangoon mills, where a modern slipway accommodating twelve gigs was added in 1938. Richard Edgar Downes-Shaw (1939–1961), Steels' Superintending Engineer, has written of gig-building—

A fully-equipped workshop produces all finished work and we buy only raw materials, the construction and repair work being carried out by Burmese and Chinese carpenters under European supervision. The boat-building is conservative in the extreme. Chinese carpenters have a rooted objection to working to a paper plan and insist on drawing out their cross-sections full size, usually on the floor of their houses. Any difficult construction question, therefore, requires to be gone into on hands and knees, with much moving of cooking pots, clothes and even children from the relevant portion of the 'plans'.

The gigs were normally sailed, and with a favourable wind were remarkably fast. In the best conditions they could keep pace with the Irrawaddy Flotilla Company's launches. They were rigged with a single big sail, and their crews, predominantly South Indian river men, were extremely skilled at handling their ungainly craft in the crowded waters of the Rangoon River. Under adverse conditions, the gigs were rowed with sweeps or towed along the bank by the crew of nine.

Jungle buying, as it proved its attraction and its strength, cut out the mill broker. In the system's first year, 1930, Steels' jungle purchases totalled a million and a half baskets. By 1937 the quantity had reached thirty-one millions, equivalent to some 470,000 tons of milled rice. In 1931 operations were hampered by the Burma rebellion, and it was thanks entirely to a loyal staff that paddy buying was possible at all. On one occasion, indeed, a buying station clerk and his subordinates captured a gang of rebels intercepted while trying to steal paddy.

Another benefit from the jungle buying system was the considerable scope for promotion for Burman head clerks which it opened up. Here were men who, having been trained within the organisation, had acquired sufficient experience to take over charge of buying areas from British Assistants. In the main they responded with great ability.

The all-important benefit to 'Beeloogyun's' peasant, of course, was prompt payment for his crop whenever he chose to sell. There was more that he might not so easily recognise in the efforts made to improve the quality of his crop. In the Government seed farms improved strains of rice were being evolved, but little interest was shown by the growers for whom there was no guarantee that improved quality would command a higher price. This was where Steels' Jungle Buying Department came in by encouraging the cultivation, on a large scale, of paddy suitable for Europe in areas where only poor-quality grain had been grown before. This was followed by their appointment of special buyers who spent their time selecting, and paying premium rates for, the improved grains.

To effect the prompt payments which this and other demands of the jungle buying system required, cash was essential but banks were few and far between. Thus Assistants, and even quite junior messengers, would set out with sacks full of bank notes to pay out to sellers of paddy. It says much for the integrity, loyalty and morale of humble Burmans and others that, though their own salaries may have been no more than fifty rupees a month, they were entrusted with cash of perhaps a thousand or more times that amount—and never absconded.

In this catalogue of benefits flowing from jungle buying, there is a lacuna that is best filled by drawing again on the writings of J. B. Clark—

It may be interesting to give some idea of what the day's work in the jungle consists. In the early mornings the Assistant has office work to do and mail to reply to, and also visits from brokers and paddy owners living near his headquarters. The state of

"The Stolid Child of Nature"

Steels' First Jungle Paddy Buying Station, Henzada—1930. J. B. Clark is seen right of centre

Steels' Jungle Paddy Buying Station, Ngaputaw

Steels' Lower Poozoondaung Rice Mill, Rangoon, as burnt out—1906

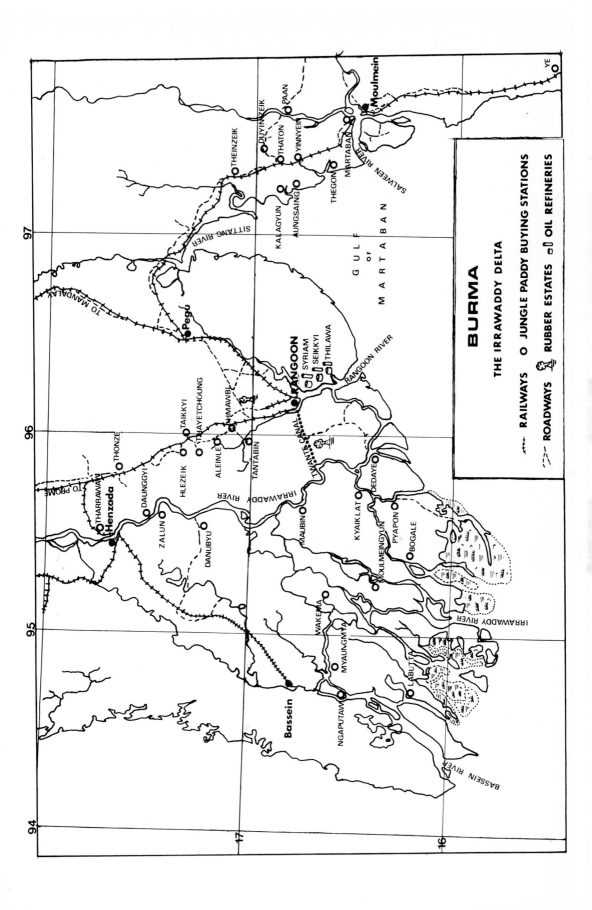

BURMA

THE IRRAWADDY DELTA

RAILWAYS   O JUNGLE PADDY BUYING STATIONS

ROADWAYS   ⚙ RUBBER ESTATES   ⬤ OIL REFINERIES

Moulmein

YE

PAAN

DUYINZEIK

THATON

KYINNYEIN

THEINZEIK

MARTABAN

THEGON

KALAGYUN

AUNGSAING

G U L F

O F

M A R T A B A N

SITTANG RIVER

SALWEEN RIVER

TO MANDALAY

Pegu

RANGOON

SYRIAM

SEIKKYI

THILAWA

RANGOON RIVER

TAIKKYI

HLEGU

HMAWBI

THAYETCHOUNG

TO PROME

THONZE

TANTABIN

ALEINLE

HLEZEIK

TWANTE CANAL

DEDAYE

THARRAWAW

Henzada

DAUNGGYI

ZALUN

DANUBYU

IRRAWADDY RIVER

MAUBIN

KYAIKLAT

PYAPON

MOULMEINGYUN

BOGALE

WAKEMA

MYAUNGMYA

LABUTTA

IRRAWADDY RIVER

Bassein

NGAPUTAW

BASSEIN RIVER

97

96

95

94

17

16

Steels' Lower Poozoondaung Rice Mill, Rangoon, as rebuilt

the market is discussed, the day's news and many other subjects. But in a short while the Assistant and his head clerk have to leave on tour. If it is a big area with poor communications they will probably be travelling by speedboat, but a speedboat is not the only conveyance used, and in various places almost all known methods of transport in Lower Burma are employed—pony, pony-cart, bullock-cart, sampan, canoe, car, bus, railway, launch and even 'shank's mare'. . . .

On arrival at a buying station news of purchases, market rates, competitors' activities and general information is supplied by brokers, traders and the station clerk. The Assistant's experience and knowledge of local conditions will help him in sizing up the situation, and he must decide on what orders he will give for fresh buying. He also has accounts to settle with brokers for paddy delivered, station stock sheets and cooly hire bills to check, samples and paddy stocks to inspect, delays in loading to deal with, and measuring and transport instructions to give to the station clerk. . . .

As far as the jungle people are concerned, one day is as good as another for a job of work, but the Assistant must push on to the next station, where he has the same routine to go through. And so on throughout the day. If he is lucky enough to be back before dark and there is a club in his headquarter town he may have a game of tennis. Then a quick change and into the office again, where he has more interviews with his brokers, his day's accounts and correspondence to deal with, and returns to make to head office. . . .

Now, from the paddy fields and the deltaic waterways, we come to the mills and their colourful history.

Burma's rice-milling story goes back as far as 1864, when a small mill was built on the Poozoondaung creek near Rangoon. Two more had been added by 1867, and by 1872 there were twenty-six, including William Strang Steel's first. Of this latter it is written that it was "built in 1871 by Mr. Strang Steel as a cargo rice mill to which white rice milling plant was added in 1888. Mr. Strang Steel enlarged the mill in 1895, when it became the glory of all the rice-milling units in Burma, with a production of 1,000 tons cleaned rice in twenty-four hours. It was burnt down in 1906 and subsequently re-built." Cargo rice consisted of one part paddy and four parts roughly hulled rice.

All mills at this early time were located on the Poozoondaung creek, which linked the Pegu District's then predominant paddy areas with the port of Rangoon and its ocean-going vessels. In 1884 a railway line was opened from Rangoon via Pegu to Pyuntaza in the Sittang river valley. A year later it was carried on to Toungoo. By 1889 it had reached Mandalay, and be it noted how hard on the heels this was of the end of the Third Burmese War in 1886. In 1893 the railway had been extended as far as Myitkyina in the far north of Burma. This opening up of the country attracted the interest of a growing number of firms in the rice-milling business. With a rapid advance of the paddy-growing area westward from Pegu, additional supplies were soon converging on Rangoon southward via the Hlaing river and eastward from the delta via the Twante canal. The role of Rangoon as the world's premier rice port was assured, while her largesse was plentifuly spilled over into the other ports of Moulmein, Bassein and Akyab, all of them providing outlet for the expanding paddy acreage, and at each of which Steels had mills from early days.

The exclusiveness of the Poozoondaung creek as the hub of Rangoon's rice milling was challenged as soon as the flow of paddy to the port fanned out in the manner described. It was not long before mills were springing up along the Kanoungtoe, Kemmendine and Dalla creeks and, by the outbreak of war with Japan, Kanoungtoe had outstripped them all.

The earlier mills were fuelled on wood or coal, but by 1882 a husk-burning furnace had been perfected and, obviously, reduced the cost of milling substantially. In the presence of so much combustible material, however, fire was ever the enemy of the rice miller and the list of mills destroyed over the years is a long one.

The best of the mills were the product of the architect's drawing board and the design engineer's workshop. William Strang Steel's first on the Poozoondaung creek had been designed and built by an engineer, Mr. Daniel Layburn, who had followed him from service with Gladstone Wyllie. Outside the conventional circle there was infinite variety, of which only a few examples can be mentioned.

There was the mill built in 1902 by Harjee Mohamed Esoof and sold to Steels during the rice boom of the 1914–1918 war. It was powered by the salvaged engine of an old paddle steamer which sank in the Salween river. There was the combined rice and saw mill erected near Moulmein by William Strang Steel in 1873 on the site of an old ship-building yard. The juxtaposition made possible the use of firewood left over from saw milling by day as fuel for running the rice mill at night. There was the mill that failed in 1876 because of the bankruptcy of the City of Glasgow Bank. There was the mill, if mills have souls, that must have known nothing but bewilderment. Built in 1882 by a Scotsman, James Gibb, it passed into the hands of a Frenchman named Dumont. Successively thereafter it was sold to Maung Po Myin, Crisp & Co., Maung Po and, in 1890, to Harjee Mahomed Hady. He, after some additions, leased it to M. M. Ispahany & Sons. The property was finally bought by Steels who dismantled it. There was the mill of improbable parentage. Built in the early nineties by a well-known Moulmein lawyer, a Briton, it burnt down shortly afterwards and was rebuilt. In 1916 it was again burnt out, and that was the end of it.

The millers were British, Indian, Italian, German, Danish, French, Dutch, Chinese, Japanese and, of course, Burmese. At the outbreak of the First World War, the German millers in particular held a strong position, with many big mills in their hands. However, after the commencement of hostilities, the German mills were taken over by the Custodian of Enemy Property and subsequently sold to British millers. Steels acquired those which had been owned by the Burma Rice and Trading Co. Ltd. and formed them into a separate group as the Burma Company Limited, a combination whereby Steels became the largest of the Burma millers and shippers with a total milling capacity of 5,500 tons of cleaned rice daily.

In between the wars, the Germans tried to regain their position in the Burma rice trade, and many of the smaller mills were supported by German buyers who set up their own buying offices in Rangoon. Intense competition developed from their effort to fight the virtual monopoly of the British group, and it was nearly ten years before a compromise was reached whereby Steels and their associates in the business took over the work of buying for the German millers.

At the outbreak of war in 1939 there were some seven hundred mills in Burma to deal with a paddy crop of about eight million tons. It was far too many— indeed milling capacity was about three times the crop—but the rice-milling business was regarded as a 'bandwagon' by many small traders who sought to clamber aboard. By a process of rationalisation, Steels had been reducing the number of their mills until only the twelve most efficient remained. Even so, this mere 1.7 per cent of the mills handled some 44 per cent of the crop.

There were five stages to the milling process, only briefly here to be described as—First, the cleaning of the paddy, by riddling it to remove stones and miscellaneous adherents, and then, by suction fanning, to take out lighter impurities. Second, the hulling of the paddy, that is the removal of its husk by passing it from centre to circumference between the working faces of two dressed discs, the one stationary the other revolving. Third, the milling of the resultant *loonzain* (rice in the pink 'underwear' that remains after hulling) which, by another friction process, removes the bran—this time in the annulus between swiftly revolving cones and their wire-clothed casings. Fourth, the polishing by a somewhat similar but less abrasive revolving cone process (strips of sheep skin or buffalo hide taking the place of wire cloth). Fifth, the grading by a process of sifting that took out broken or small grains to the extent required. The quality of the end product stood to be varied by mechanical adjustments in any or all of the last three stages.

The milling picture is not complete without a reference to the development of parboiling. The process involved the steeping of raw paddy in hot water tanks for a day or two, followed by a drying out on sun floors or in hot air-heated towers. Thereafter the paddy was stored as usual until it was given a milling that needed only to be light. The advantages of the process were firstly the retention of the vitamin B and mineral elements that largely are lost when rice is well milled (with the consequent risk of *beri-beri* where diet is ill-balanced), and secondly the characteristic that parboiled rice, once cooked for consumption, is slower to sour than straight-milled rice.

Back in the London Office was a rice samples room wherein, once a week, on a long counter, were laid out samples received from Rangoon of current purchases, millings and shipments destined for various markets and diverse tastes. A young Assistant, whose training this was for a career in oil, recalls with pleasure the presiding genius of his day, William Thom Milne (1906–1933), whose other claim to fame it was that in 1907 he was one of a two-man team that opened an office at Bangkok, Steels' first establishment outside of Burma. Willie's sometimes deceptive mildness of manner endeared him to all, and somewhere in the shadows there must linger yet the infinite sadness of such verdicts as 'too many weevils'.

From the Rangoon mills the bagged rice for export was loaded into 'cargo boats' designed specifically for the passage between mill and ocean-going vessel. They were massively built of teak to withstand a life of grinding and bumping, and were sheathed below the water-line with zinc sheets as protection against the very destructive and plentiful teredo worm. Carrying capacity varied from fifty to three hundred tons, and the crew, who lived aboard, from seven to twenty.

The ships which have carried rice down the Rangoon River and across the seven seas for so many years would provide a wonderful pageant if they could be paraded. As an item of his research, on which the present writer has already relied, J. B. Clark produced a list of shipping in the Port of Rangoon on 17th

March 1886, and it is gratefully borrowed as an appendix to this story.* As Clark himself speculates—"One wonders what the reactions of the Director of Shipping, Rangoon, or the owners of the Bibby, Henderson or British-India Shipping Lines would be nowadays if ships were detained in Rangoon for months at a time as was the case in 1886!"

These, of course, were all sailing ships, and typically they loaded for India, Ceylon, Malaya, China, Japan, Australia, Mauritius, South Africa, the United Kingdom, Germany, Poland, Czechoslovakia, Holland, Norway, Sweden, Denmark and South America. Here is a catalogue of fickle markets in a hard, unyielding trade—markets ever ready to turn from Burma to Indo-China, Thailand, Java or America; or even to start growing their own rice if price or quality did not match local ideas. It was a trade strewn with casualties, and there is perhaps some truth in what a well-known German miller said to a member of a European firm in Burma, who went to Hamburg in 1921 to try to obtain his business—"You have lost this Agency by two days and for your sake I am glad, as it would have broken you in two years' time. The Devil made the rice business and the Devil controls it."

Lest any be asking "why all this agony and sweat over rice anyway?", let one man answer with a nice blend, hopefully of fact, certainly of salesmanship. In his address inaugurating National Rice Week in Washington in March 1955, Mr. J. Norman Efferson said this—

> Rice, not wheat or corn or potatoes or milk, is the most important food in the world. Rice supplies the major food requirements for about one half of the world's population. This single food makes up from 70 to 80 per cent of the entire food intake in many countries.
> Rice is not just rice. It has more glamour and more varieties than the orchid family. There are more than 9000 [sic] different varieties of rice now being produced around the world. Rice can be blonde, brunette or redhead. It can be scotch, bourbon or saki. It can also be rice honey. In addition, it tastes good. What orchid can claim as much?

It is a fortunate circumstance that Captain Joe Cattanach, who gave up command of the Henderson Line's *Burma* in 1926 to take up the post of Shore Superintendent Rangoon, contributed to Steels' *House Magazine* in 1949 a first-hand account of the day of the 'tall ships'. There follow some extracts from what he wrote under the title "Clippers and Rice"—

> My first introduction to Burma was in the Monsoon season of 1902 when I arrived there as Chief Mate of a sailing ship—the *Queen Mab*.
> There were many windjammers in Rangoon in the late nineties, but by the beginning of the present century they were reduced to only a few. Messrs. Jas. Nourse's ships were frequent visitors and used to carry rice and Indian emigrants to the West Indies.
> On my first visit I well remember our ship being hove to in the Bay of Bengal about 200 miles S.W. of Table Island during a cyclone, and I remember also, when aloft looking for our landfall, picking up the masts of a wrecked steamer west of the Krishna light vessel. That vessel was the ill-fated s.s. *Comorta* of the British-India Company, and I believe she was lost with all hands, including a large number of Indian labourers. . . .
> We started our voyage from London in December 1901, and were seventeen days (including Christmas and New Year) beating down the English Channel bound for Durban with a general cargo which consisted mostly of provisions for the Army. From Durban we came to Rangoon in ballast and were chartered by a firm named Zaretsky Bock & Co. to load a cargo of rice for two ports in South America—Talcuhama and Valparaiso. . . .

* See Appendix No. C.

We lost several members of our crew (in Rangoon)—sick men left in hospital and deserters, and on the eve of sailing we were still three men short. However, two stowaways came to light—one an ex-Tommy and the other ex the Railways, both looking for adventure. They found it! They both turned out to be good men, but the ex-Tommy was evidently a rolling stone, and deserted us at Costa Rica a year later. . . .

I never thought in those days that eventually I should join a Company trading to Rangoon and settle down as a shore *wallah* there; but it happened so.

After the disappearance of the Clippers—and the world lost much by their going—the day of mechanisation arrived irresistibly, first the coal and then the oil burners, helping, alas, to lay the foundations of the pollution of the waters that has now become one of mankind's paramount concerns. As agents for the major shipping lines operating in and out of Rangoon, Steels' rice export programme met little in the way of chartering problems; but by this time Steels stood virtually alone of all the exporters who had striven so long to share their survival in the trade. The German miller's Devil had done his work.

*   *   *

Steels' involvement in the Burma rice trade created wider-ranging ripples, some briefly at least to be mentioned. Continental Europe, particularly Germany and Poland, was from early days a substantial market for rice; and, until the 1914–1918 war deprived them of their identity, German companies had been active millers in Rangoon. As far back as 1906, a consortium of Burma millers and shippers, including Steels and in association with a German company, Mohr Brothers, had formed in London 'The General Rice Company' (which came to be known as 'London Shippers') with a subsidiary, the 'Allgemeine Reisgesellschaft', owning and operating a mill in Hamburg, followed later by a second mill in Breslau. The object of the association, basically, was to canalise, in the interests of the Burma market, a large paddy and rice import business which otherwise might have been placed elsewhere. In fact, pre-1914, 'London Shippers' secured some eighty per cent of the Continental business, while their activities were extended to the manufacture of starch in Poland.

1914–1918 closed the book, and the impounding of German mills in Burma was suitably reciprocated by the seizure of 'London Shippers'' mills in Germany. However, memories of a successful pre-war venture spurred 'London Shippers' in 1920 to revive the project, this time as 'The New General Rice Company', and again to build a mill at Hamburg. This mill outstandingly justified itself before, in its turn, it was demolished by the Royal Air Force in 1944.

These recurrent deterrents did nothing to diminish the resilience of the dedicated rice men, whose enthusiasm spans national frontiers. Determined to recover from the devastations of the war, as early as in January 1947 an agreement was signed between the Neue Allgemeine Reisgesellschaft and A. Luthke & Company, an old-established firm of German millers, to tackle the post-war rice trade together instead of in competition. Both companies having had their mills destroyed, the agreement provided for the re-building of a joint mill which was completed before that year was out, and the partnership has flourished in the post-war era.

Thus quickly can the scars of war be healed. Indeed, Steels' historian of the second century will have much to say about the company's resurgence as a powerful force in the world's rice trade. No longer, however, does the feedstock come from Burma. The Hamburg and Breslau mills have operated post-war on the exportable surpluses of Thailand, Surinam, Egypt and North America. Time was when 'rice to Burma' would have been as nonsensical as 'coals to Newcastle'. Yet, to quote from an Australian Government publication—"a small consignment of aid flour was made in 1972 in view of the shortage of cereals and flour in Burma. It is expected that a larger consignment of flour will be sent in 1973." *Eheu fugaces*!

* * *

To Cuba in 1935 came 'London Shippers' through the on-the-spot management of Steels. At the time, Burma and Siam were the major suppliers of rice to the Republic of Cuba, the largest and most populous of the West Indies islands. For reasons much like those which had prompted their European venture years earlier, the consortium had purchased a rice-milling business in Havana, the 'Compañia Primer Molino Arrocero de Cuba'.

The war of 1939–1945 put a stop to Asian rice reaching Cuba, and although the business made great strides in fostering the cultivation of Cuban paddy, the mainspring of the venture had gone and the business was sold to American interests in 1953. The subsequent history of Cuba has endorsed the move, wittingly or unwittingly, as sound.

* * *

In the United Kingdom, in 1915, Steels acquired an interest in a London rice milling company, Carbutts, which in 1928 became wholly-owned as Carbutt & Co. (1928) Limited. By that time the main steam-driven mill had been electrified, and a year or two later the business was expanded by the purchase of a mill in Hull. The Managing Director of Carbutts from 1928 to 1954 was the James McCraken who, earlier in this story, described the coming of the *Loungzats* to Steels' old Lower Kanoungtoe mill in 1906. In 1951 he wrote of Steels' acquisition of Carbutts that—"Our initial survey of U.K. markets had shown with what indifference the public treated Burma rice—and this after all the trouble we had taken in selection and milling in Burma! Import figures proved that only about 21 per cent came from Burma and India. This seemed absurd: the more we examined samples of foreign rice in favour here, the more we were convinced that Burma could supply the wherewithal to allow of our turning out rices of better value." (In 1951, be it noted, McCraken's 79 years old miller, Tom Goddard, "showing little sign of wear and tear", had been with Carbutts since 1886. The company was not short of experience!) Since the end of the Japanese war and the loss of the Burma market, the London operation of Carbutts has been closed down, though milling continues in Hull.

* * *

No matter what the future may hold elsewhere in the same line of business, this story of Steels and rice in Burma is ended. Its significance for the history of

44

its times should not be underrated. In the forests of Burma, Steels stood in the shadow of The Bombay-Burmah Trading Corporation. On the oilfields they were out-topped by the Burmah Oil Company. In the rice market they were supreme —and it was here that the rules of survival were the toughest of all.

A last look, before we go, at 'Beeloogyun's' peasant cultivator. He is an old man now and nearly blind. Since being deprived of his piece of land by legislation that promised much but lacked fulfilment, he has lived on sufferance in his married daughter's house in a small village on the bank of a river down which the launches with the red and white ensigns used to glide. His food, rice of course, is brought to him by a small grandson. There is not much of it, but therein lies merit, apparently, because it comes from something called a people's shop. The boy is his closest friend, and delights in his re-telling of stories such as the one about the *bo-gyi* from the launch who so drastically but successfully treated the snake bite on his foot. The old man thinks, sometimes, of his long-gone oxen. Was his treatment of them such as to impair his chances of a happier re-birth in the hereafter? Perhaps he should have built the small pagoda he used to contemplate on the rising ground at the end of his field? But, and he sucks sadly at his pipe, it won't be done now.—It won't be done now.—

CHAPTER III
FORESTS AND TIMBER

Valid or otherwise, it is some criticism of Steels' west to east posting system in their Burma days that young men were sent out to fill vacancies of chance rather than of choice. The youngster in the London Oil Department, finding himself in a rice mill a year later, might well know in his heart, later yet, that the forests were his real *metier*. By that time an apocryphal barrier known as 'the Staff programme' tended to militate against a transfer.

The forests called for a special type. Physical fitness and mental resilience were vital. Ambition must needs be irrelevant, for the jungle, normally, did not lead to the Boardroom. The forester lived too near to the soil and too far from the market place. Yet, of all, here were the men who really had the opportunity of knowing the land they lived and worked in; of speaking the language of the country; of becoming naturalists, artists, philosophers and counsellors of simple people who had nowhere else to turn for lack of the means or the education.

Where nationalistic policies now dictate—as perhaps they must if they are to succeed—that the evidence of the British connection be expunged rapidly and by whatever means, the last pockets of resistance will be found in the forests. Here will survive stories, passed down from father to son, of acts of justice, compassion and friendship. On humble walls will hang, damp-soiled and insect-eaten, fading photographs of *bo-gyis* who were trusted and loved because they earned both.

Steels came into the teak business as early as into the rice, but then only as exporters of what others had extracted and milled. Thirty years later, at the turn of the century, the timber firm of J. W. Darwood & Company determined on an intriguing change of course. They abandoned forestry in favour of founding and operating the Rangoon Electric Tramway & Supply Company. Curiosity goes unsatisfied. One is tempted to speculate that this was nineteenth century management's conception of an imaginative leap into the twentieth.

For Steels, the 'old hat' of Darwood's discarding was their own acquisition of the forest leases, the elephant herds, and the forest staff of which Darwoods required to divest themselves. Here indeed was mutual obligement rare and remarkable; and, as if that were not enough, Darwoods' senior forester to cross the road was Bertrand Theodore Petley (1900–1930) who, in defiance of earlier analysis, was the first and only forester to become Chairman of Steels.

In their beginnings, the forest Companies—of whom the Bombay-Burmah Trading Corporation were the acknowledged pioneers—must have had much to grope for. Teak there had always been, but the technique of its felling, extraction, milling and marketing was something to be rationalized by trial and error under conditions that often were vile. The demand for this remarkable timber, of course, was unlimited. Indeed there are records of teak shipment from Burma to India going back as far as the early part of the eighteenth century.

The absence of guide lines for the earliest of Steels' recruits is apparent from the writing of Frederick Hanmer France (1902–1927)—"Of forestry and sylviculture I knew something, having been assistant agent on a well-wooded estate in Surrey, but I was warned that 'the Government chaps look after all that' and 'you will be shown your job when you get out there.' So I was given a few sums to do, just to prove I was no arithmetician, taken on as the first covenanted member of the forest staff and given a month of reading up old forest diaries and correspondence to get the atmosphere."

Forests cover more than half of Burma, but teak seldom comprises more than a tenth of the trees to be found in a typical area, and this can mean that there is no more than one mature teak tree to the acre. Maturity implies a tree of not less than six feet girth at breast level, when the height is likely to be between 80 and 100 feet and the age up to 150 years.

Every teak tree in Burma was the property of the Government. None could be felled—even if it stood in your own garden—without the necessary authority. The Government pursued a realistic policy of conservation, and an area from which mature trees had been fully extracted could not be entered again for thirty years. The teak forests were leased by the Government to such companies, indigenous or foreign, as could satisfy the requirements of strict legislation and had the means, financial and physical, of meeting their commitments.

Officers of the Government Forest Department supervised the killing of all teak trees chosen for felling. This was done by 'girdling' them conveniently near to ground level, the process requiring that the bark and the sapwood be fully severed all round.* Thereafter the trees had to stand for at least three years so that they be dried out and seasoned sufficiently to become floatable.

Typical teak terrain was hilly and broken by *chaungs*. This and the inconsistent spread of the trees marked for extraction militated almost entirely against access by mechanical methods of haulage. Under bad conditions the elephant, and under not so bad the buffalo, were the only practicable instruments of transfer from logging site to such main streams or tributaries as had the flowing potential in the rainy season to carry the logs down to the rivers.

At the outbreak of the Second World War, Steels' elephant herds totalled about 700 animals out of a working population in Burma of about 5000. The training and the care of his elephants became a personal responsibility for the forest Assistant. Much has been written about these astonishingly sagacious creatures. Their training had to start in early youth if, when they came onto full load at the age of 18 to 20, they were to know what was required of them. By that time they would have attained a height of about seven feet at the shoulder and a weight of three to four tons. In many ways they were delicate beasts, easy

* See Appendix No. D.

47

victims to infectious diseases such as anthrax, against which they were regularly inoculated; and to vicious boils and harness sores arising usually from bad management. They needed a bath with the greatest regularity, and the calls of feeding and sleeping were such as to limit their working effectiveness to six hours a day ending, normally, at noon. They required a personal staff of two men per animal during their working life, which ended in their sixties. With all these limitations the elephant in Burma was a priceless gift of Nature for which, in their specialized role, man has yet to devize a substitute.*

At the end of their years-long death throes, the teak trees were felled at ground level, mostly by saw, and the forest Assistant visited them with his logging crew. The bole of the tree, having been cleared of creepers, was measured and hammer-marked to show the points at which it would later be sawn into logs.

Logging is an art calling for skill and experience. Unsoundness in over-mature trees must be sensed and appraised: irregularities of shape must be taken into account. These observances can make a considerable difference to the value of the timber obtained from a tree once it has been sawn into logs. (For the statistically minded be it recorded that the largest teak log extracted from the forests of Burma measured $82\frac{1}{2}$ feet in length with a centre girth of 10 feet, and it cubed over ten tons—approximately the weight of three elephants.)

After logging, a double hole was cut at one end of the log, through which was passed a chain. This would be coupled to the elephant's harness and the log then dragged to a stream bed whence flotation became possible in the rains, or to a depot whence carting by buffaloes—up to ten or twelve to a cart—would be practicable. The drag in either case might run up to ten miles.

During the rains, between May and October, rises flushed the tributaries and larger streams. Elephants without harness followed the rises down-stream, breaking up jams by pushing the logs forward until they reached a larger stream. Thence the logs floated out to main river where they were collected by villagers and made over, for a fixed fee, to the rafting staff of the lessee. Up to this point, individual logs might have had two or three years of seasonally interrupted travelling from stump.

In the major rivers, notably the Irrawaddy and the Chindwin, the logs were assembled at rafting depots into 'sections', generally of about twenty logs' width. Eight or ten sections were then made fast fore and aft to form a raft. On the raft would be built sufficient grass huts to accommodate the raftsmen, their wives, children, dogs and miscellaneous possessions; and off they would go. If the starting point were an Upper Burma depot, the motley crew had a journey of up to five months in prospect—say 400 miles to the Government measuring station at Mandalay, where the logs were assessed for royalty, and then 500 miles to the log depots at Rangoon, where the 'craft' would be made over. Thence all con-cerned were provided with rail tickets back to the villages, where they settled down as 'landlubbers' until the next rafting season came round. Who is to say that we have not here some approach to a perfect way of life?

At the log depots on the Rangoon River the rafts were broken up and the logs graded. They were then re-rafted to the mill or to the auction depot as required. The royalty paid on teak in Burma was assessed at so much per ton

* See Appendix No. D.

48

More ways than one of shifting teak logs

More ways than one of shifting teak logs (cont.)

More ways than one of shifting teak logs (cont.)

More ways than one of shifting teak logs (cont.)

Building a teak raft

of 50 cubic feet, according to source and conditions of extraction; and over later years it provided an average of about thirteen per cent of the total revenue of the country.

Onto the bare bones of description we should now fuse the flesh of personal involvement. Carl Edgar Rosner (1927–1942), one of Steels' Anglo-Burman forest Assistants, has provided this lively account of a by no means untypical occasion.—

The monsoons had not favoured us so far, and except for a few insignificant showers we had had very little rain, nothing but heat and more heat. Extraction in the Shwedaung area had been completed and all logs were in stream, nicely arranged and only waiting for the water that would take them out. The *ounging* herds were standing by patiently. . . . I, personally, could do no more. Nevertheless, the motionless ranks of logs seemed to be accusing me of bad staff work . . . and as it was of no use trying to fight the accusers, the next best thing was to run away, so off to Tatlwin to see how the logging of next season's outturn was getting on. Tatlwin is a peaceful spot—a small village with a streamlet beyond it on one side of the bungalow and paddy fields on the other. The logging was going according to schedule. All very soothing . . . and so to bed.

Midnight and a storm. The sky was black with clouds and a gale blew. Lightning and thunder soon followed, flashes as vivid as daylight that rent the sky and deafening claps of thunder that made the earth shake, and at last the rain, welcome rain. . . . With a light heart I got back to bed and dreamed pleasantly of rises, elephants *ounging* and logs jostling one another as they were borne along.

In the morning it was still coming down in torrents, the paddy fields were a sheet of water, and the road to the village was impassable. All day it poured incessantly with not a moment's respite. Reports reached me that all streams were in spate and that not even elephants could ford them, while by evening reports were of houses having been washed away. This was beginning to look serious. I had taken stores for only a couple of days so could not afford to be marooned, but, even worse, was the fact that the bungalow, which was on low-lying ground, stood a good chance of being washed away. And so the order was back to Shwedaung in the morning if possible. The pleasant dreams of the previous night had taken rather a nightmarish turn. . . .

Next morning there was little change, the rain coming down steadily. The two short routes that are used ordinarily were impossible as both cross large streams. We decided on a longer route where the streams to be crossed are small, and set out. The first stream was little more than waist deep but the current was swift. There was no trouble in crossing but a certain amount of excitement, as everyone shouted advice to everyone else, including the elephants who entered wholeheartedly into the noise and fun. A mile along brought us to another alleged stream, but this was rather a different matter. The stream(?) was an enormous stretch of angry water that raged and fumed, tumbled uprooted trees over one another and crashed them into the banks as it went tearing along. No crossing this. The elephants were of the same opinion. They took just one look at it and then started giving one another advice in no uncertain voice and not in a spirit of fun. Nothing to be done but to return by the way we had come and then to try another longer but less hazardous route. Mid-day found us about halfway to Shwedaung. We had staggered through the slush and waded through the streams and had even done a bit of swimming, but we had managed to get along. We were tired out, however, so called a halt and ate a welcome breakfast miserably. The leeches in the meantime had been breakfasting off us heartily. Puttees would not keep them out, so I shed the puttees, rolled my socks down over my boots and every few minutes scraped the leeches off my leg with a knife. . . . The snakes weren't having such a good time; they seemed to be concentrated on getting somewhere, even as we were. . . . They wriggled past us when we waded and swam alongside of us when we had to swim. They didn't appear to be hostile but we didn't do anything to encourage friendliness. . . .

On again after the breakfast interlude still in pouring rain. At long last we came to the Government path, but this did not mean that it was plain sailing. Some of the bridges had been washed away while others were leaning over drunkenly, and we had to do a bit more wading through the streams. . . . We hurried along and came within sight of the bungalow. There it was smiling its welcome to us from the top of the ridge. But the path—where was it? Completely gone! Either washed away by the stream or

49

else blocked by landslides. As we watched, this process of washing away and blocking continued. However, we had come so far and we were going to get to the bungalow. Nothing for it but to crawl along the ridge as best we could. This required skilled mountaineering but we set to it, holding hands and cutting steps with *dahs*. At the landslides we sank up to our waists in slush and had to pull one another out by brute force. The elephants roared and protested, but did their part manfully, or should I say elephantfully, and at last we were there.

But life was not always thus hard, as the forester himself would be the first to admit. There were the marvellous cold-weather days that made of Upper Burma an earthly paradise. Easy is it to recall the jungle fowl shoots that belonged to relaxed week-ends in camp. There were those long reaches of shaded water where the mahseer lurked, the swampy rice fields that harboured snipe, the dawn-dim lakes where the geese gathered. For the more ambitious there were the bison, the tiger and the wild elephant, though shooting of these animals was carefully controlled where it was not of necessity. For the naturalist there was just about everything.

There were the laboriously cleared polo grounds and race tracks at the Forest Headquarters towns, which usually were Government District Headquarters as well; the golf courses, of a sort, and the club tennis courts—all providing relaxed recreation under conditions of freedom from an excess of your own kind. There were the periods of rest from hard slogging, or of recuperation from fever, to be spent at 'Ingleston', the Forest Department's home-from-home amidst the pleasantness of Maymyo, or in one of the Company's bungalows at Kalaw. Few would say of this life that a better took its place when it was so abruptly terminated.

It is fashionable today to preach—Anglo-Saxon historians not excluded—that the story of British Imperialism is one of harsh exploitation of illiterate, unprotected peoples. Let us look at one example of how the process worked.

The Thoungyin Valley lies between Moulmein and the Thai (Siamese) border. The inhabitants are mostly Karens. The valley and its flanking hills are as beautiful as anything to be found in Burma, and life there seemed to hold a special quality. This peaceful way came the Japanese invaders in 1942; and at Kawkareik, near the border, they met and wiped out their first opposition in Burma—a platoon commanded by a hastily commissioned officer who knew the area well, Raymond Edward Hall (1930–1942).

The Thoungyin was first leased to Steels in 1906, having previously been worked indifferently by Government contractors. To get teak extraction under way in an efficient manner, it proved necessary to bring men down from Upper Burma leases along with their elephants. Here, and elsewhere in later years, it was painfully learnt that a policy of transferring labour never worked—be it in teak extraction or on oil exploration or otherwise. If it wasn't because of demoralization away from the home-village environment—leading to laziness and crime—it was non-resistance to the local strain of malaria or some other reason. There is perhaps something in the oriental temperament that disqualifies a man for separation from his natural background.

Early on, therefore, started the laborious process of mustering new elephant herds, educating local contractors and sub-contractors to a new role, and training young Karen lads as *oozies* and *pejeiks*.

The guiding hand in all this was that of Gordon Hundley (1907–1950)—known to the Karens as 'Saw K'pi', the butterfly. It is his account from now on—

In the office we collected English speaking Karens from the west of the Dawnas. Our greatest difficulty was the illiteracy of local contractors and forest staff. In the majority of cases orders had to be passed by word of mouth, and so the idea came to teach the staff and villagers to read and write.

Sgaw Karen *Thin-bon-gyis* (spelling books) were introduced by the gross, school 'readers' followed and the rapidity with which the local people learned to read and write Karen was truly amazing. Then the idea of introducing English speaking Karen lads from the Moulmein schools developed and results exceeded expectations. Our felling camps took on the aspect of evening schools, and our elephant staff spent all their spare time studying reading and writing. As they were all now recruited locally they disseminated this desire to learn throughout their villages. Thus appeared another effect, for the desire did not stop there, and those, who were striving after this first education, thought of their younger brothers and sisters. Wages were saved and we remitted monthly school fees to pay for these relatives in the Moulmein schools. These relations did their time at school, returned to the villages and either entered our service or worked with their own folk amongst our contractors. This is briefly the story of how literacy came to the Thoungyin Valley. . . .

In 1949, in the London Office, grieved by the tragedy of post-war conflict between Burmans and Karens, Hundley wrote to the Directors—

My ambition has always been to return to my friends in Burma, both Burman and Karen, and help them to come together, the only solution. Under today's conditions I believe that if the Burma Government would accept my offer to return and do what I could with my knowledge of both peoples—and my known friendship with them all—I might help to obtain this solution.

The state of his health, if nothing else, forebade and he died within a year. His obit in the *House Magazine* records—

. . . his last wishes were for his ashes to be taken and scattered over the Kamakala Gorge of the Thoungyin River in the presence of his Karen friends so that the spirit of 'Saw K'pi' would again wander over the country and be amongst the people whose memory he so greatly cherished.

So passed a 'tool of Imperialism'; but who would be surprised one day to learn that 'all the trumpets sounded for him on the other side'?

Earlier on we had a look at the qualities required in a forester. As with the men, so with the women. A forester's wife, if she and her husband were to know happiness, had to be a special person. More than for others did her way of life entail a degree of involvement in her husband's activities. She had to learn to live with solitude and sickness, with discomfort and sometimes distress. Fortunate was she if her nature marched with Nature; if her fingers were green or masters of a paint brush or a pen; if she relied not at all on gossip and small talk, and did not resent that her daily conversation was in a language not her own. It seems fitting that one of these ladies should contribute to this story.

Elsie Wellard is the widow of Norman Edward Kersey (1919–1940). Before her marriage she was a singer of distinction. The goldfish bowl of modern living will probably deprive the chronicler of 2070 of the pleasure of reproducing anything quite as pleasing as her memories—

My ten years in Burma were very happy ones and the jungle and its people, its pagodas and its palaces have left a lasting impression on my mind so that now I can still conjure up the vividness of the scenes without too much difficulty and, I hope, without too much sentimentality.

It was with very great sorrow that I heard soon after my return to England from Australia in 1946 that Mepale had completely disappeared. I suppose that I was happier in the isolation of the Thoungyin Forest than ever in Mandalay, even though Mepale was three days' journey from Moulmein and visitors were rare, so that it was quite exciting for us whenever the guest bungalow was occupied. Once we were fourteen months without having another European in the compound.

I wonder what has happened to the people and the babies who used to live in the compound. Perhaps they have forgotten us, and all we tried to do. I had hopes that a small hospital would be built at Thingannyinoung, five miles from Mepale, but this unfortunately never materialised. There was a good deal of sickness among the large population spread throughout the frontier tract bordering on Siam and what little help we were able to give by distributing simple medicines was but a drop in the ocean, so such a hospital would have been invaluable.

Our life even in the Rains was pleasant enough, though I can remember still how the incessant battering of the rain and the croaking of the bullfrogs wore down one's nerves. The great excitement of the day was to measure the rise of the water by stakes at the bungalow steps. . . .

The roof of the bungalow was of small hardwood tiles, earth oiled and red ochred to preserve them and to give them a rich red colour which was particularly pleasing seen through the haze of the smoke from the cooking fires. The verandahs were open to the weather and to any of the people who cared to come up the steps, and I remember how intrigued they were by the radio, run off a six volt car battery which had to be carried to Kawkareik for recharging. . . .

The garden was my particular job, and a great joy to me. With gesticulation and laughter I made, I think, as good a success as was possible with a Ghurkha durwan as *mali*, his second in command a Karen, a Mugh cook and a Shan boy, all of us more enthusiastic than knowledgeable. But at least one saw quick results there, and I still haven't got used to the length of time which seed germination takes in England. Beans were my great hobby in the Mepale garden and in the rains I was able to grow about fifteen flourishing varieties.

Before our arrival the use of an airgun in the garden had scared the birds away, but they soon returned when they found that they had nothing to fear and they were a joy to watch. Tea in the garden was the signal for them to come for crumbs, and the cook had orders to make cake for them daily. There was much chattering and argument while they took their baths in the bird bath which had been cast, I think, by Noel Boyt. The most amusing were the Hornbills, which arrived each year to nest in the banyan tree. How these huge birds could balance on the most slender branch was a thing I could never understand, and it was wonderful to see them pick up a fruit and then roll it down their throats where it was possible to watch its progress until it reached the stomach. Their journeys to and from the nest were very regular, and their wings made a wonderful surging noise as they flew.

Much of my husband's work was done on raft transport, and the other day, when seeing the Kon Tiki film, I lived again the many tranquil hours I had spent floating down the frontier river, the Thoungyin, on rafts very similar in construction and design. Here I learned to float the leaves of a creeper down over the small rapids and pools to hook mahseer—that wonderfully sporting fish—a method often more successful than the most intricate fishing gear.

My last memories of the Thoungyin are on my final journey over the hill after I had returned hurriedly to pack up my belongings. I stopped to watch the jungle fowl feeding by the side of the road and, looking over the valley across to the hills, could see three pagodas standing out white and clear in the evening sunshine. Farther down the road as dusk fell we stopped to watch a family of sambhur, their eyes like lamps in the headlights of the car. All was then peaceful and beautiful, and I could not guess that only a little later war was to ravage the area—and that I should never see it again.

In our earlier passage down the Irrawaddy with the rafting community we stopped short at the mills. On arrival there, the first treatment for each log was a thorough washing to clear it of the slime, stones and other debris collected during its tumblings and driftings. Each log was then assessed by an expert sawyer. If straight and sound, the normal practice was to cut it up to yield a square. If otherwise, the consideration became that of obtaining the largest sections possible, length normally being more important than breadth. If decking timber was required—and this was teak's function *par excellence*—the log would be opened up in slabs of the required width and then sawn to the specified thickness. Enough said, perhaps, to show the scope for experienced sawyers in the limitation of waste. Down to a section measuring one inch by half an inch by eighteen inches teak was commercially marketable. Of the little left over, the sawdust went to the furnaces and the remainder was sold as firewood.

It is surprising to be told of teak—that most nearly impregnable of all timbers —that it has an enemy in a moth called the bee hole borer. This creature lays its eggs in the bark, and the larvae, when they hatch out, bore into the bole and can cause extensive damage. Nothing but the best will do for the bee hole borer: it is found only in teak country.

Nevertheless, stories of the durability of teak are legion. An example is provided by the thirty-gun ship *Java* built of teak in Calcutta in 1813. After forty years' service as a man o' war, she was sold to a London company who used her variously in a sea-going capacity until, at a date unrecorded, she berthed at Gibraltar. As recently as the outbreak of war in 1939, she was still there doing duty as a coal hulk. Perhaps she is still around.

At this point we leave the success story of teak to resurrect memories of a forest venture that failed largely through lack of official recognition of the problems involved.

In 1920 Steels were encouraged by Government to interest themselves in hardwoods, a line hitherto tackled in a hand-to-mouth manner only by Indian and Burmese millers lacking the capital necessary to establish themselves in the teak business.

In 1921 Steels took over a small sawmill at Swa, in the Toungoo District, and by 1924 had replaced it with a modern Canadian mill. An original two feet gauge railway track was replaced by ten miles of metre gauge line carrying American rolling stock. American logging methods—reinforced by the calling in of experts in the handling of the machinery—were introduced, but the comparatively sparse stands of timber and an inexperienced labour force made for a continuous struggle. Local demand for hardwoods was soon satisfied, but the United Kingdom and other overseas markets were slow to accept unfamiliar woods of unknown character.

Another forest area—the Yonbin Reserve, east of Pyinmana—was acquired in 1928 to increase the proportionate production of *Pyinkado* timber, the cream of the crop; and a fine forest operation was built up. Even so financial results were disappointing. Round logs had to be railed 60 miles to Swa, and the converted timber a further 175 miles to Rangoon. The heaviness of hardwoods made for excessively high freight rates and an ultimate selling price of more than twice that ruling for teak.

Government refused to help by reducing their royalties or by subsidizing freights, and every attempt by Steels to alleviate these and other adverse factors failed. The last straw was the world-wide depression in 1931, when it was reluctantly decided to cut losses by closing down the project and selling the expensive plant for the scrap prices that alone were obtainable under the conditions.

So ended a venture that cost Steels £250,000 and, largely through Governmental intransigence after their original encouragement, killed all prospects for Burmese hardwoods in overseas markets.

When war came to Burma, he who spoke the language, could identify and interpret the sounds of the jungle, say what was and what was not edible, and deduce the location of water by instinct or experience—this man had a military value beyond any normal yardstick of measurement. He was likely to start the day as a civilian and bed down as a captain in a blacked-out bivouac.

During the years that followed, four of Steels' foresters were killed and four others won the Military Cross. These latter included two Anglo-Burmans, representatives of a small national community who, because they could usually pass as Burmese, were often called upon to do so in circumstances calling for the greatest courage. It would have been fitting had one of their number won the Victoria Cross.

Here, typically, from James Noel Carpenter (1937–1954), is a fragment from a longer account that conveys something of what was asked of these young men—

> We left on schedule but en route were blown off our course and arrived late over my supposed Dropping Zone. Plane lights had been blacked out and the door opened with me on the threshold and my men lined up behind all ready to jump. One look at the panorama below assured me that we were not at the correct place. I ordered the plane to carry on and circle around in search of the correct location which I could recognize from the aerial photograph still fresh in my mind's eye. An argument ensued, with me against the entire crew of the plane, as to the correctness of our position. This was very trying and not good for the morale of my men, so I decided that one risk was as great as another and asked my men to volunteer to follow me despite the fact that we would land blind. There were no dissensions so out we went. Our frequent circling had of course aroused the suspicions of the locals so that half an hour after landing, and before we had collected all our parachute containers with the bulk of our stores and equipment, we were almost surrounded by unfriendly Burmans. We got away with the ruse of burning all our chutes, causing a huge fire which attracted our enemies to it, whilst we slipped away and marched practically non-stop throughout the night. I, my second-in-command and two others sprained our ankles. Two others landed on the tops of very thorny trees and had to be cut down, causing them much pain in the process. Our progress was consequently poor. . . . From a villager we caught, we were alarmed to hear that we were only three miles away from a force of some two thousand Japs, and thirty miles away from the intended dropping place. Did I curse the Air Force?

Apart from the senior staff casualties, a number of the Burmese forest staff were killed out of loyalty to their calling. *Singaungs*, protesting against the overworking of their elephants, were in some cases executed out of hand on the accusation that their objections proved their pro-British sympathies. The elephants themselves paid a heavy price. Victims of bombing and ambush, or of gross overwork, they died lingering, uncomprehending deaths in some hundreds: and yet, when the Fourteenth Army returned to rout the invaders, the extent to which their devoted custodians brought elephants out of hiding or slipped them away from the Japanese makes a remarkable story.

After military victory, the writing for the timber companies was soon on the wall. It was the case just before the war that many of Burma's forest leases were due or nearly due for renewal. Nationalisation of the Government by that time had reached a stage which, of itself, ensured that negotiations would be difficult and protracted. The Japanese invasion, however, prompted Government to concede indefinite extensions of all expiring leases until such time as renewal negotiations could be resumed in a peaceful atmosphere. It was a meaningless, tongue-in-cheek formality.

Having had the opportunity, after the war, to assess their stupendous losses, it was not surprising that the forest lessee companies had to tell the Government that they would be quite unable without assistance to raise the capital necessary to re-establish this large and valuable industry. Eventually Government agreed to provide such assistance, and the five surviving timber companies formed themselves into a consortium on the general basis that profits after rehabilitation would be shared equally between the firms and the Government of Burma. Before the ink on this agreement was dry, however, Government announced a far-reaching policy of nationalisation, the forest and timber interests being high on the list. Compensation was derisory and, after garnering what was left to it, the consortium was dissolved. Thus ended the long association of British companies with the teak forests of Burma.

So, from the northern forest areas of Myitkyina and Bhamo, from the Central Burma leases in the Mandalay, Pyinmana and Prome Districts, and from the Southern Burma forests of the Thoungyin and Tenasserim, Steels' flag was struck, and a skilled team of foresters was broken up and dispersed. Twenty-five years later, the question of who has gained by all this is best left to such historians as cannot be accused of bias or personal involvement. Here let there be no more than a generous tribute to the thousands who were left behind to serve other masters in their own land.

*   *   *

Steels' entry into the forests of Guyana (then British Guiana) was on the basis of a contract for five years—time enough to make an impact; not long enough to establish the human relationships that were the forester's strength in Burma. In 1947 the company was commissioned by the Colonial Development Corporation to open up a timber (mainly greenheart) business with its office in Georgetown, the capital, and its forest base at Wineperu on the Essequibo river some fifty miles from its mouth.

The project, under the style of British Guiana Timbers, involved surveying and mapping a large area of country, plotting the species and density of the trees to be found therein and cutting the necessary extraction roads, for which latter purpose it was further necessary to open and operate a quarry to provide the soling stone. Until Steels' arrival, the most accessible forests had been creamed of their best timber, trees with minor defects had been left standing, roads had been cut without maps to show whither they went and no overall extraction plan had been evolved.

At Wineperu it was necessary to clear an area of bush for the establishment of a base camp and depot. For work in the forests, tractors had to be imported for the haulage of logs to depots, cranes for the loading of the timber lorries, winches and overhead cables at the waterside for the transfer of the mainly unfloatable logs from the lorries to the pontoons that would take them down-river to a rail-head en route to a saw mill to be built in Georgetown on the Demerara river, which debouches into the sea about fifty miles east of the Essequibo. The project called for the posting to Guyana of a team, about a dozen strong, of Burma-trained forest, saw mill and office staff.

For a little 'brush work' we borrow from an account written by Christopher Penrose Morley (1937–1952)—

Our '*Tawtha*' (Jungle *Wallah*) starts off with an initial difficulty, his large tracts of unbroken forest contain no villages or inhabitants and are consequently pathless and practically unknown. He has to start by importing all his labour, of which there are two types, the Amerindian who is indigenous to the colony and who is a jungle man acquainted with its lore, or the African negro from the town who has to learn it the hard way and who is rarely happy in it. Unfortunately, of the former there are comparatively few and they live in the north-west corner of the colony far from the site of his operations. A special effort has to be made to recruit them and bring them down. They are a well built race of Mongol origin and look very like Kachins, are good workers who can be left on their own to do a set job, are well mannered and react to good attention. . . .

For exploration work and tree identification they are ideal but are not up to the heavy manual labour of which the African is capable. Consequently both must be employed on their respective jobs but must not mix in camp or at work, for the Amerindian is ephemeral and quickly upset, and if this happens, will pack up and go off in a night. The African has a very different outlook on work; with few exceptions he does it as a means of acquiring a sufficiency of money in as short a time as possible to enable him to carouse it all in Georgetown where there is bags of fun and rum . . . much of this can probably be blamed on the casual system of employment in the country where there has not been the mutual respect of the employee and the employer as was known in Burma. Through his employment being so transient the African has generally had little chance to get to know his employer. But when he does start to get acquainted he begins to like discipline as for the first time he knows where he is, his respect grows and with it his manners which can be most genuinely effusive. . . .

The forest, he finds, has none of the interests of the Burma jungle; it is frequently very thick and nearly always completely featureless. The latter was clearly divided up into watersheds: how he cursed those steep hills but their ridges did delineate the country. Here the country is lightly broken up but in no clear-cut pattern, the streams, or 'creeks' as he must now call them, frequently disappear into swamps and then drain away the same way as they came in. There are no paths and no easily defined ridges, all exploration must be made on compass lines cut straight in order that they may be traced at a later date or plotted. Any maps there are are of the sketchiest and too frequently are more of a snare and delusion than a source of assistance. '*Tawtha*', who never used a compass in Burma, would now not move a yard without one. . . .

Does it rain, does it not! But not of the civilised monsoon variety when '*Tawtha*' was ready and expected it. Here with the heat and the large rivers the sky becomes a sponge which has to relieve itself at least once a day. . . .

And that delightful cold weather tour when even the dingiest 'zayat' (rest house) took on the appearance of home with the familiar table, chair, bed (and office box) laid out in their usual order by Maung Ho Din. No Maung Ho Dins out here! No service which was more than service with a smile. With no elephants, mules or carts to carry the baggage, touring is an ordeal where the minimum is taken and where any ministrations are by a hand unskilled in all else but that of opening a tin. . . .

Steels' five year term ended with the project well and truly launched and established. Several members of the staff were seconded to the Colonial Development Corporation for further periods to ensure a smooth succession.

*　　*　　*

The Rondo Plateau of Tanzania—it was Tanganyika at the time of Steels' association with the country—is to be sought in the extreme south-east of this larger-than-Burma territory. Some seventy miles to the south is the border with Mozambique; and some sixty miles to the east is the Indian Ocean, approached from the Rondo through the small ports of Lindi and Mtwara. Dar-es-Salaam, Tanzania's principal port, is over two hundred miles northward.

The plateau itself could be the setting for a Rider Haggard story—a flat top, about 2500 feet above sea level, so nearly isolated from the surrounding country by almost vertical cliffs as to ensure that the company-built road from the mill on the plateau to rail-head eighteen miles distant would ever double as a surveyor's triumph and a traveller's hazard. To this strange place, in 1949, came Steel Brothers (Tanganyika Forests) Ltd. under a contract with the mandated Government of the country to open an extraction and saw-milling project. The timbers to be harvested were Iroko and Mninga, the former having something in common with teak—to the extent, indeed, that teak saplings were brought in from Burma on an experimental basis. Though rainfall on the Rondo was not heavy in the eyes of a staff used to Burma conditions, the trees are of considerable size and their canopy, viewed from the air, can appear to be almost unbroken for many miles—this despite an almost total lack of humus to overlay the sand in which the trees are rooted.

The brief reference to Burma conditions invites a record of the fact that "U Aung Myint, U Chit Sein and Hla Win, who are the senior members of our Burmese staff, are on secondment from Steel Brothers & Co. Ltd., Rangoon, and have completed 24, 11 and 23 years' service respectively, of which $5\frac{1}{2}$ years have been spent here at Rondo." These secondments were no act of 'political' lip service, but the deployment to best advantage of established talent—a teaming of Europe and Asia in Africa of such a quality as nationalism deplores and human survival probably requires.

Africa is notably elephant country, but the animal is not used domestically to anything like the same extent as his Asian cousin. It is not that he cannot be trained for work but the nature of the terrain that explains his relegation. So much easier is it for mechanical extraction methods to be used in African conditions that the elephant has never emerged as the answer to a forester's prayer. He can be seen as a carrier but seldom as an artist in the sagacious exercise of brute force.

Despite the immense scale on which everything in Africa is drawn, fourteen years of efficient operation brought Tanganyika Forests to the point where all marketable timber on the Rondo had been worked out, and, with nothing else on offer, the African venture was closed down.

So, after more than sixty years, Steels' footfalls died from the forest floor.

* * *

As a sweetener to an otherwise sad ending to this story of the forests, there can be added the following extracts from recorded history—

From *The Borneo Story* by Henry Longhurst (being the story of the first hundred years of The Borneo Company Limited from 1856 to 1956). The time is December 1951—

> In Sarawak . . . the Company has come out of its corner to engage in a third round with the forest. Though one of two 'trial' elephants brought from Siam before the war had died, it was clear that the climate suited them perfectly well and that elephants were almost as indispensable in Sarawak as in Siam. Unfortunately, however, wartime losses had caused not only Siam but also India and Burma to prohibit their export. Looking nearer home, the Company turned to Chipperfield's Circus and bought five beasts aged eleven to seventeen years, at which age it was believed that they would remember nothing of their circus life when they reached the forest.
>
> Advice having been taken from Elephant Bill,* they were shipped on the upper deck of the P & O liner *Soudan*, together with rations including, among other things, 500 bales of hay, three cases of rum, and ten pounds of Epsom salts. Refreshed by 200 banana stems at Penang, they were transhipped at Singapore—after a good deal of trouble from one called Myrtle—and safely slung off at Sarikei fifty-two days after leaving Southampton. Their first action was to swim across the river, nearly half a mile wide, and get bogged the other side.

From Steels' *House Magazine*, Vol. VIII No. 1, June 1952—

> Though we, ourselves, can claim no direct association with the export of five circus elephants last December, we are at least indirectly interested by reason that it was Edward Wright who had the job of caring for them on the voyage to Borneo, where he and they have gone to work for the Borneo Company. *The Times* saw fit to devote a Fourth Leader to the occasion. . . .

In Vol. IX No. 1 of the *House Magazine*, Edward Wright (1936–1948) has given his own, colourful account of this improbable mission. The preliminary 'staff work' was erratic at least in respect of one detail. In the context of the "three cases of rum" (which, genuinely, were intended for elephant consumption), Ted writes—"It was my 'misfortune' to discover towards the end of the journey that my last remaining case was one of gin and not of rum!"

Where would one go today for a training that qualifies a man to chaperon five elephants half way round the world by sea?

---

* Lt. Col. J. H. Williams, O.B.E. (Bombay-Burma Trading Corporation), author of 'Elephant Bill'.

CHAPTER IV

OIL

From firmly established bases in the rice mills and teak forests, Steels' venture into the speculative quest for oil must have savoured of rashness to some at least of those who guided the Company's passage at the time. One can almost hear the thumping on the Boardroom table of those who would maintain that 'we should stick to what we know'. The adventurous prevailed nevertheless, and the outcome is now a matter of colourful history.

In 1908 Steels formed the Indo-Burma Petroleum Company to take a fifty per cent interest in an existing oil business founded, and actively presided over, by a remarkable man.

Abdul Karim Abdul Shakur Jamal was an Indian, born in Jamnagar State of humble parentage. He had emigrated to Burma and started in business as a *dukan wallah*, a stall-holder in a Rangoon bazaar. He was, however, a man of ambition with a great talent for organising and, amongst other things, he had branched out by buying and leasing drilling sites at Yenangyaung. He had even had the nerve to engage an ex-Burmah Oil Company Drilling Superintendent, Mr. Percy Corey, to drill for him. In anticipation of success, fortified by Corey's local knowledge, he had further embarked on the erection of a 2000 barrels-per-day Refinery at Seikkyi on the Rangoon River some miles down-stream from the Capital. This extensive plunging had exhausted his cash and his credit, and the approach to Steels was the result.

The future Sir Abdul has been described by Thomas Taylor McCreath (1903–1961) as "a very able man, but an inveterate optimist and gambler". If the wisdom of alliance with such a character was ever questioned at the time, it is arguable now that Sir Abdul's qualities were no more than pre-requisites to success in the prosperous oil man at any time anywhere.

Be that as it may, on 7th August 1908, John Baines Harman (1898–1920), Steels' first oil man, came ashore at Nyaunghla to face a flooded five mile ride to Yenangyaung. His charge, as he described it, comprised "two wells producing, no offices, a store and one bungalow", but events were to show that Jamal had read the stars aright and that Steels had backed a winner by joining him. The second of the two wells, on being deepened to only 1200 feet, came in as a major producer. It flowed uncontrolled down a nearby *chaung* for three days before being connected in to a hastily-assembled pipe line, whereupon it was throttled back to 2000 barrels daily, this quantity being the capacity of the improvised line.

The problems created by the bringing in of, and handling production from, a well of this calibre from a starting point of total unfamiliarity with the oil game were varied and perplexing. Jamal's refinery had come on stream, to the accompaniment of many mistakes and minor accidents, to produce—at about 500 barrels daily—two grades of kerosene and paraffin wax. Petrol at this time was no more than a tiresome by-product.

However, the triumph at Yenangyaung soon uncovered an ugly truth. The refinery was quite incapable of running at anything approaching its rated capacity, thus imposing a heavy restriction on the rate of production at the field. This was most unwelcome in view of the consequential and permanent loss to be expected of oil that would flow to the offsetting wells of competitors now being drilled. It was agreed as a matter of urgency that additional refining plant must be procured to rectify the position.

The new plant arrived and, having been erected with great expedition, proceeded to demonstrate its embodiment of all the weaknesses of its predecessor. Nevertheless, the two combined provided a rate of throughput that would take care of the foreseeable future. What to do about the pile-up of current production was the immediate problem.

Though sites for petroleum installations in Calcutta and Bombay had been acquired, at neither did I.B.P. yet have bulk storage or the attendant pipe line systems from tanker moorings to tin factory. Nor indeed were there tankers to carry petroleum products or tin making facilities to pack them. The only place where kerosene could be packed was Seikkyi, and the daylight capacity of the tin factory was 8000 tins daily. Under conditions that must have meant stomach ulcers for maintenance engineers, the output was raised to 20,000 tins working round the clock. Tins were stacked to the roofs of all available I.B.P. godowns, supplemented by a hired rice godown which, not having been designed with petroleum regulations in mind, was a lively hazard in conditions where leakage was serious.

Then, as McCreath relates—

> . . . the shipping problem began. We chartered a B.I. ship, the *Scindia,* to take a cargo of tins to Calcutta. She arrived there with oil in the hold to a depth of seven feet and the Port Commissioners of Calcutta advised us that if such a thing happened again our shipments of oil would be barred entry. . . . We had asked London to charter small steamers with 'tween decks for future tin shipments. The first ship sent out on a six months' charter was the *Morven,* a 6000 ton cargo steamer with one particularly shallow 'tween deck. A more unsuitable vessel could not have been found. It was heartbreaking to see the huge hold, like an enormous tank, and to think of what was going to happen to our tins. However . . . we designed and built several teak 'tween decks into the steamer at a cost of Rs.40,000. . . . These decks solved the problem of tin transport. Outturns were reasonably good and our worries over the construction of the decks were rewarded at the end of the charter when we sold the timber at more than it cost. It was well seasoned with oil and seemed to be popular in consequence.

In anticipation of completion of the installations at Calcutta and Bombay, with Chittagong soon to follow, the tanker *Perlak* was chartered from the Anglo-Saxon Petroleum Company on a hire basis. Of her arrival McCreath recalls—

The installation at Calcutta was completed in record time and when the *Perlak* arrived in Rangoon we were able to load her with bulk oil to the plimsol marks and despatch her for that port within 36 hours. This was a great triumph. The only disappointed man was the Dutch skipper who had anticipated a long rest with plenty of gin in Rangoon, as he had obviously been informed that our installation would not be ready for a long time.

The year 1912 marked the completion of the flurry of activity thus described. The teething troubles of Seikkyi had been resolved, the Indian installations were in full operation, and, in succession to the *Perlak*, I.B.P.'s own tanker, the *Shwedagon*, sailed up the Rangoon River to take up a service with the company that was to last for over forty years.

At this point we should take a look at the manner in which the Steels/Jamal partnership had been developing. They were still equal shareholders in I.B.P., but the division of function had become distinct. Steels managed the oilfields, the refinery and the Indian installations, while Jamal handled the selling agency both in India and Burma. This arrangement worked very well as Jamal had built up an excellent sales organisation in both countries. In 1922/3, however, whereabout Jamal himself died and his family ran into crippling financial trouble through injudicious speculation on the Rangoon rice market, Steels took over the selling agency. The managers of Jamal's sales offices in India came over to Steels, a fact which ensured not only a smooth transition but also a strong, ready-made selling organisation for there were some outstanding men of business among them.

Reverting now to Yenangyaung, the oilfield was remarkable enough to merit some description. During geological ages the reservoir rocks had fractured, leaving the oil free to migrate upwards to wherever it could find lodgement. Thus the structure held oil at many levels, in accumulations of varying volume and, in the main, with the pressure that had provided the motive drive dissipated. Oil seeping to the surface (the translation of *ye-nan-chaung* is water-smelly-creek) had proclaimed the presence of a remarkable substance, with lubricant and inflammable properties, long before the European arrived with his drilling equipment.

Since early times, the Burmese had been producing oil from hand-dug wells from depths of down to about a hundred feet, and their right to continue to do so was preserved when applications for oil prospecting leases started to come in. It was a remarkable sight to see a hand-dug well, about four feet in diameter, being worked against a background of wells pumping on the beam from perhaps two or three thousand feet. As often as not it would be a husband at the bottom of the hole, hand-filling a four-gallon kerosene tin, while his wife at the surface pumped air down to him through a pipe linked to a mask covering his nose and mouth.

The owners of these small, circular well sites, the *Twin-zas*, had the option of leasing them to the oil companies on a royalty basis; and it was not uncommon for three rival companies to be producing from separate wells located within an area equal to that of a tennis court. The wells, as may be imagined, numbered about two thousand; and the field as a whole looked like an impressionist artist's conception of a forest of leafless trees.

In its heyday the non-Asian population of Yenangyaung, mostly British and American, numbered about six hundred. History, alas, does not always march with progress. The final picture of Yenangyaung in this story comes from the pen of Field Marshal Sir William Slim, describing the events of April 1942—

> After visiting Yenangyaung at 1300 hours on the 15th April, I gave orders for the demolition of the oilfield and refinery. It was essential that they should not fall intact into Japanese hands. . . . A million gallons of crude oil burned with flames rising five hundred feet; the flash and crash of explosions came as machinery, communications and buildings disintegrated; over all hung a vast, sinister canopy of dense black smoke. It was a fantastic and horrible sight.

*　　　*　　　*

Success at Yenangyaung had not blinded I.B.P. to the need for proving new reserves of oil, for further leasing prospects at Yenangyaung were nil. Harman records that "every effort was made from the start to obtain new productive territory elsewhere. Ondwe, our first 'wild cat', gave only hot water and Kyaukwet, after weeks of negotiating for, gave nothing." When success did come (and production from Yenangyaung was then down to about two hundred barrels daily from over a hundred wells) it was as a heady succession of discoveries—at Indaw, some miles inland from the Chindwin River in its upper reaches; at Lanywa, *under* the Irrawaddy some forty miles up-stream from Yenangyaung; and at Khaur, in the far remove of what was then the Punjab of India but today is Pakistan (though this latter, for politico-practical reasons, was to burgeon as The Attock Oil Company). Confusion will be the less if these ventures are described individually rather than chronologically.

The Lanywa oilfield was unique. It had long been the thesis of I.B.P.'s geologists that the oil-bearing structure lay wholly under the Irrawaddy, either as an extension of the Chauk field, which the Burmah Oil Company was developing successfully on the east bank, or as an independent anticline. This interpretation, fortunately, had been rejected by the B.O.C. geologists, the chief of whom is alleged to have undertaken to drink every drop of oil the I.B.P. got out of Lanywa!

In 1913 the I.B.P. theory had been tested by the drilling of a well on a sand-bank exposed during the low-water season. This well had not reached the postulated oil-bearing horizon before the river rose and called a halt to operations for that year. Then disaster struck when a river steamer ran foul of and carried away the well-head. There followed an official enquiry at Government House in Rangoon, presided over by Sir Harcourt Butler, the Governor of the day. Among those called to give evidence was an old friend of Steels on the Irrawaddy, Captain Frank Musgrave of the Irrawaddy Flotilla Company, from whose contribution to Steels' *House Magazine* in 1941 the following is extracted—

> Sir Harcourt then said—'Captain, was it not you who tried conclusions with the pipe which was left in the middle of the river?' I replied that I did happen to be the unlucky one but that whereas, fortunately, there was no damage done to the steamer much was inflicted on the pipe. Sir Harcourt's next question, smilingly put, was—'What did the Burmah Oil Company pay you for shifting the I.B.P. pipe?'

Despite the Governor's levity, the enquiry resulted in Government's placement of a ban on any renewed attempt at off-shore drilling not backed by what were bound to be very costly protective measures. After the war of 1914–1918, daunted by such a formidable restriction, I.B.P. fell back on an inevitably less attractive alternative and drilled five wells above the high-water mark. Of these the first yielded a small, non-commercial quantity of oil and the fifth some gas from a deeper horizon. These unprofitable results, nevertheless, were enough to steel the Company's resolve to drill off-shore again despite the cost of the protective works insisted upon.

The measure adopted took the form of a guide wall built out into the river from the mainland along the outer edge of the inshore sandbanks. The top of the wall had to be higher than the highest recorded rise of the river, and the whole strong enough to withstand the full force of the river in flood.

The project was submitted to the vetting of the highest engineering talent before it received Government's approval. The design required a wall one hundred and fifty feet wide at the base, forty-five feet high and fifteen feet broad at the crown. Protection of the weather slope called for a minimum thickness of two and a half feet of heavy stone facing and, running out from the toe of the embankment, an apron of stone one hundred feet wide and four feet thick. Construction started in the low-water season of 1925–1926 with a labour force of five thousand, and the original length of five thousand feet took three low-water seasons to complete. The cost was about a million pounds sterling, which in those days represented a gamble of frightening proportions.

Fortune favoured the brave, however, and I.B.P.'s seventh well, the first to be drilled behind the guide wall, struck oil in a manner that set all doubts at rest. Four subsequent extensions of the wall carried it to a total length of over two miles, but the original construction had so denuded the near countryside of suitable stone that the extensions were faced with bricks burnt in an immense brickyard established at Lanywa for the purpose. The bricks measured twelve by twelve by six inches and, as far as was known, were the biggest bricks ever burnt for any occasion. Ultimately the wall shielded from the flow of the river something over a hundred oil wells.

To begin with, of course, the wells were being drilled in water exposed to the rise and fall of the river. The wall diverted the flow: it did not dam it. As they were completed they were connected by walk-ways, while the concomitant paraphernalia of tank batteries, pumping stations, power sub-stations and so on were likewise 'waterborne'. A decision followed, therefore, to fill in the area behind the wall. To this end a diesel-electric suction dredger, the *Margaret*, was bought and, over many seasons, achieved an area of reclamation that embraced even the outliers of the oil wells and permitted a network of roads that brought every corner of the Field within easy motorable compass. For its day the whole project was a magnificent feat of engineering and the completed cost was about five million pounds.

The guide wall, though it started almost at right angles to the river bank, had had to follow a curving course that finally brought it nearly parallel with it. For all that it had made possible, therefore, the wall had narrowed the flowing width of the Irrawaddy to only a small degree—less than twenty per cent in fact. Nothing more was technically possible in this direction. Thus most of Lanywa's oil still lay under the river and its recovery called for some other technique.

This took the form of a line of wells drilled along the top of the wall itself and deliberately inclined from the vertical so that they 'bottomed' at considerable distances out under the river. Fortunately the nature of the formation favoured inclined drilling and, with the aid of special equipment, ultimate deviations of up to seventy degrees from the vertical were obtained.

Came the war, and in 1942 men who had lived with and become a part of Lanywa, a fierce grief in their hearts, 'junked' the wells and installations and moved on, with or without a backward glance according to temperament, to commit similar sacrilege elsewhere or to die on the road out. These things must be incomprehensible to those who have never been condemned to play such a role; and even though vindication was later to come, for some at least the scars must ever have remained.

After the war, in the few brief years that lay between the independence of Burma and the end for the oil companies, Lanywa came under the logical operation of the Burmah Oil Company administration across the river at Chauk. Some of Steels' and I.B.P. staff were seconded to what had become a joint venture in the mammoth task of restoring the oilfields. The last view we have of a remarkable fruition to daunting hopes mentions the new, all-weather airstrip on the reclaimed area behind the wells. This and the trans-river oil line, skilfully floated out and sunk in position by the B.O.C., smack of progressive development until one detects the spur of the security that had to be established in a rebel-dominated countryside.

*   *   *

On a day in May 1934, the juniors of the London Office were gathered about the lunch table in serious vein. The conversation was dominated by the news received that day that Douglas Brown, a young Assistant on his first *chukka*, had accidentally been killed at Indaw. Reaction ranged from prayer for preservation from such a posting to assurance of outright refusal to accept should it ever be ordered. The place, by reason of its virulent malaria, had long been of evil repute and had claimed several lives over the years.

Indaw (of the Upper Chindwin, not of Katha) was an unimaginable place because it defied total description. It could depress and it could elate. If you could appreciate natural beauty in an atmosphere of menace it was the perfect posting. If you could enjoy a threesome of bridge, there being none to make a fourth, you were well suited.

The Field had been opened up in 1911–12 by the construction of a road [*sic*] from the riverine Pantha. The first oil was struck in 1913, by which time already Indaw boasted a prolific gas producer in its No. 1 well. There was, of course, no conceivable market for the gas.

The approach to the Field from Pantha followed the worn-down bed of the Khodaung Chaung, winding so tortuous a passage between its cliffs that it had to be forded twenty-seven times in the last nine miles. Up to this point, travel in the dry season was possible by a specially geared truck. Thereafter ponies took over. During the rains the choice throughout lay between ponies and elephants, or some combination of both.

The oil and telephone lines followed the gorge; the one buried, elevated or otherwise protected against the depredations of wild elephants; the other barbed to discourage monkeys from swinging on it. Stores and equipment went in by bullock carts or elephants according to season.

Of this strange setting wrote Thomas Dunsire (1920–1948)—he having had three spells at Pantha on transfer from Seikkyi—"It was always a relief to get the periodical oil pumping finished without undue loss of oil, and fortunately enough the elephants did not destroy the line so long as there was pumping taking place". Whether, in the elephant, this argues a fear of the pulsation or an understanding of the purpose is a matter on which opinions will differ according to the degree of individual familiarity with the animal.

On arrival at Indaw, the pivotal feature of the place became apparent as the confluence of the Khodaung with two equally large *chaungs*, the Wettin and the Mawton, flowing north and south respectively. Thick jungle marched down steep slopes and halted at the water's precipitous edge.

The oil wells spanned about seven miles of the Wettin/Mawton artery, from which, scattered by veins represented by plunging tributaries, they were seldom more than a quarter-mile distant. The artery was criss-crossed by suspension bridges for foot traffic only—some of them as much as four hundred feet in length. In the low-water season these were supplemented by flimsy foot bridges across the *chaung* beds. A rough road ran parallel to the artery, and this crossed the veins by wooden bridges strong enough to carry an elephant and its hauled load. There was no wheeled transport, though a few tractors worked at *chaung* level, usually in co-operation with the elephants. Ponies were the one alternative to walking, and then only in the dry season. Where wells were drilled on very steep slopes, access to them was by railed haulageway.

The curse of Indaw was the anopheline mosquito. From the commencement of drilling it posed a serious hindrance to development and, after several deaths from malaria and blackwater, problems arose from the refusal of drillers—all Americans in those days—to accept posting to Indaw.

In 1925 an anti-malaria campaign was mounted under the direction of the School of Tropical Medicine in Calcutta, whence two Indian staff trainees were transferred long-term to Indaw. In 1929 the Principal of the School himself made the first of two visits to Indaw and laid down guide lines aimed at canalizing or eliminating mosquito breeding grounds. For years thereafter he received weekly reports from the Field Agent, whose personal responsibility it became to ensure that oiling and flushing were regularly carried out and that a minimum daily 'bag' of mosquitoes was caught, classified and dissected in the laboratory. Strict observance of routine progressively yielded a notable reduction in death and sickness rates.

Indaw was subject to occasional earthquake shocks and more frequently to climatic violence. In 1926 a cloudburst in the upper reaches of the Mawton *chaung* produced a flash flood that raised the stream level by about thirty feet in a mere ten minutes. The Agent at the time was Armour McGilvray (1915–1963), whom the present writer remembers with affection as his own first guide and mentor up-country. McGilvray received enough warning to escape through the back door of his bungalow, but he then had to keep running up-hill. From a safe elevation he watched his bungalow wrenched from its stilts, swirl out into mid-flood, capsize and sink. The Field Engineer suffered and survived likewise. On

65

the field twenty-three people were drowned. For years thereafter the shifting sands of the *chaung* beds were yielding up equipment lost on that dramatic occasion, but, among other things, a locomotive-type boiler, a workshop lathe and the office safe never did come to light.

As with the down-river fields, Indaw was 'denied' in 1942 by a small band of loyal and exhausted staff (including McGilvray, now the Manager of the Oil Department), whose only escape then was to walk to India. On the basis of meagre information, it appears to be the case today that the field is derelict and abandoned to the mosquitoes. In a countryside that soon was to become studded with Allied and Japanese graves, there comes ironically to mind a solemn exhortation that was a standard sentence at the end of all Indaw handing-over notes— "You should see that the grave of Mr. Bowman is properly cared for." He, of staff who died at Indaw, was the only one to go in high-water conditions. The others lie in consecrated ground at Mawlaik on the Chindwin or elsewhere farther down river.

*   *   *

The venture at Pyaye, which started as a 'wild cat' test for oil and ended as a cement factory, is described in another chapter. Here one Burma field remains to be mentioned—I.B.P.'s joint venture, and a successful one, with the British Burmah Petroleum Company in the Pyinma Development Company some seven miles from the B.O.C. stronghold of Chauk. The object of this equal partnership was to reduce competitive drilling since, on what was known as the Moolla block, the B.O.C. flanked both the I.B.P. and B.B.P. leases.

In these conditions it could happen that a company on one side of a lease line brought in a good producer at the statutory minimum distance of three hundred feet from the line. Inevitably the drainage area of such a well would extend across the line, so the rival company would then drill an offset well to secure its own oil. Thus would develop a 'line fight', with wells being sited tactically instead of economically. These matters came to be better ordered, but at one time 'line fighting' could be recognised from afar by the parallel march of rows of largely superfluous derricks.

The P.D.C. 'settlement', of pleasant memory for more reasons than its proximity to the Chauk golf course, was described in a letter written from Chauk in 1952— "There are a few bricks left at a couple of bungalows, the tennis court at the site of the Agent's bungalow and a few foundations; otherwise one would never have known this was once a flourishing colony." Thus is rung down one more curtain.

*   *   *

Apart from the companies directly involved, for none did the discovery of oil at Yenangyaung and elsewhere prove such a bonanza as for the Irrawaddy Flotilla Company (the 'old Flotilla' of Rudyard Kipling). As there burgeoned on the Rangoon River, some miles downstream from the Capital, the Refineries at Syriam (B.O.C.), Seikkyi (I.B.P.) and Thilawa (B.B.P.) so, for the I.F. Co came a freight opportunity beyond dreaming.

Since the year 1910, Syriam was fed by a pipeline from the Fields; but the other companies continued throughout to send their crude down by river in large flats secured one on either side of a river steamer. To the river traveller this was a most familiar sight, reminding one of a buxom matron advancing mid-pavement with her overgrown progeny one on each arm. Who gave way to whom could never be a matter for dispute.

The men of Seikkyi, unfortunately, have been reluctant chroniclers for the purposes of this story, but Dunsire, writing in the year of his retirement, has left a between-the-wars picture from which these extracts are taken—

> At Seikkyi Refinery where I was posted, the workings were a repetition of distillation units in the Scottish Shale Oil Works in the Lothians at home. . . . Petrol in those days was not delivered in bulk, it had still to be tinned and cased. These cases were made of ½ inch thick teak wood, planed, with proper dove-tail joints, and would be high-class furniture on present-day standards. . . . There was a 'Naptha' bench outside the main Refinery as a safety measure; and just prior to 1914, and possibly after this, 'Naptha' was burnt as there was no market for it and it was dangerous to mix it with the Kerosene, which gives a fair picture of the importance in the life of petrol or Naptha as it was called in those days, i.e. say 35/40 years from being a nuisance to attaining a value like gold. . . .
>
> The Refinery plant was more or less the original type of plant used from the earliest days, namely elevated shell stills and cast-iron pot stills for coking the residue. This coke for many years only found a use in cookhouse fires, and therefore accumulated rapidly. . . .
>
> Wax manufacture and candle making have improved as regards type of plant used, but the principles remain the same. . . . The Tin factory made double-seam tins, small drums and petrol cans. In due course single-seam tins were established and have proved themselves to be cheaper to make and strong enough for the work they have to do. . . .
>
> Residue oil from the Pantha Refinery came down in the early days in kerosene tins to be turned into lub oil at the Refinery. . . . I went up to Pantha first in 1922 and found a small edition of the old type of plant, without of course any wax extraction plant. . . . The Tin factory eventually closed down, and all the oil came down in the river tanker *Chintank*. . . . Latterly only a staff in the Indaw Field remained and Pantha was closed down.
>
> . . . Another leave Home and I.B.P. were then at low ebb, low oil production, cuts in salaries, etc. The B.O.C. Refinery staff had one walk round our Refinery to check up the inventory made out to hand over to them, as oil production had reached such a low level that separate refining became uneconomical. Fortunately Lanywa proved a winner shortly after that and it was like a blood transfusion. New plant lists were drawn up, and from 1930 onwards a Refinery of modern type emerged. . . .

Alas for the "Refinery of modern type"! In March 1942, the present writer, in a military role that he had never remotely contemplated, found himself charged with the inconceivable task of covering the demolition of the refineries to prevent their falling into the hands of the advancing Japanese. Here is what he had to witness from his weapon pit forward of Syriam—

> I knew what was about to happen, of course, but I could not find it credible. Here were these monstrous, costly conglomerations of tanks and towers, pumps and power houses, with all their diversely ordered banks and swathes of pipelines, about to be blown sky high. With them would go all the 'no smoking' and 'fire danger' signs that rendered the conception unthinkable.
>
> Promptly at noon the first of hundreds of storage tanks suddenly erupted under the compulsion of a vast ball of fire that soared and mushroomed into the sky from its bowels. Before the pursuing surge of black smoke engulfed them, I could see fragments of the tank shell that must have weighed tons floating earthward through the heat like sycamore leaves. At some time the crescendo of that initial explosion must have reached me, but already I was stupefied by the succeeding eruptions and soon was deafened

by the roar of flames and the rapid 'crump' of succeeeding detonations. Down-river I could see Seikkyi and Thilawa leaping into self-destruction.

Sickly fascinated, I watched the inverted mountains of solid black smoke writhing and billowing upward and outward from each pyre until, with an imagined gesture of familiarity, they linked arms with each other and swung and surged hither and yon to wherever unsullied, open sky still afforded accommodation. Sometimes, at the base, I could still see the eruption and glow of fresh sacrifices to this awful god of total destruction, but gradually the darkness of the pit took over.

The enemy radio described this day as one of more hot air over Rangoon than usual.

*　　　*　　　*

Nothing in this story of Steels and oil is more richly documented than the career of that wonderful old lady, the tanker *Shwedagon*. Perhaps it is that for sailors in particular, lacking the facilities for gardening and golf, an hour or two with pencil and paper provides a diversion of contrast from the tedium of daily routine.

New from her builders, owned by I.B.P. and under the command of Captain Pat Gentles, *Shwedagon* sailed up the Rangoon River in 1912 to cope with the crisis of plenty at Yenangyaung which has already been described. Over many years she was a familiar friend to Steels and I.B.P. staff posted at Rangoon, Seikkyi, Chittagong, Calcutta and Bombay; and, for the landlubber, what better road back to health after sickness was there than a round trip in this hospitable hull? Her officers were welcome guests ashore at all ports always. It was not permitted to them to forget that they were of the family.

During two world wars *Shwedagon* was detached to play an active service role, dodging the Germain raider *Emden* in the first and, in the second, quartering Australian, New Guinean and South Pacific waters in the Allied cause. Captain Tom Goodbody, since 1927, was her commander during this latter period, and his wartime O.B.E. was a distinction that he must have been glad to share with his ship and her company. He clearly lost his heart to Australia for he retired to and died there.

Shwedagon's Chief Engineer for many years, Robert Rendall (1925–1952), gives this account of her final—and only—homecoming—

> Word of *Shwedagon*'s arrival at both Swansea and Sunderland had gone round with a vengeance. Press reporters saw to it that her fine record—perhaps unique for a tanker which for most of her life had carried motor spirit—was given a lot of publicity, and representatives of the builders (W. G. Armstrong Whitworth & Co. Ltd.), the fabricators of the engines and boilers (The Wallsend Slipway and Engineering Co. Ltd.), the Admiralty, etc., were soon aboard to express themselves as astonished at the condition of everything that they saw after such long and arduous service in both peace and wartime. The B.B.C. also took a hand in the publicity and I had the honour and pleasure of broadcasting short talks about the ship on both the Home Service and Light Programme 'Radio Newsreel'.
>
> It will be of interest to record that to the end the engines and boilers of *Shwedagon* were those with which she was originally fitted out. The triple expansion engines gave excellent service throughout, never once broke down at sea, and no more eloquent tribute to the quality and workmanship which went into the boilers is possible than to say that it had never been necessary to use the spare tubes supplied at first commissioning. They were still in the ship, untouched, when she was handed over to Messrs. Thos. Young.

The Lanywa Oilfield and Guide Wall (stage 2)—1932

The Yenangyaung Oilfield—*circa* 1920

The Indaw Oilfield—1935

"Scorched Earth"—the death of Seikkyi Refinery—1942

S.S. *Shwedagon* (1912–1952) on her final voyage

Khaur Well No. 1 "blowing in"—1915

Morgah Refinery

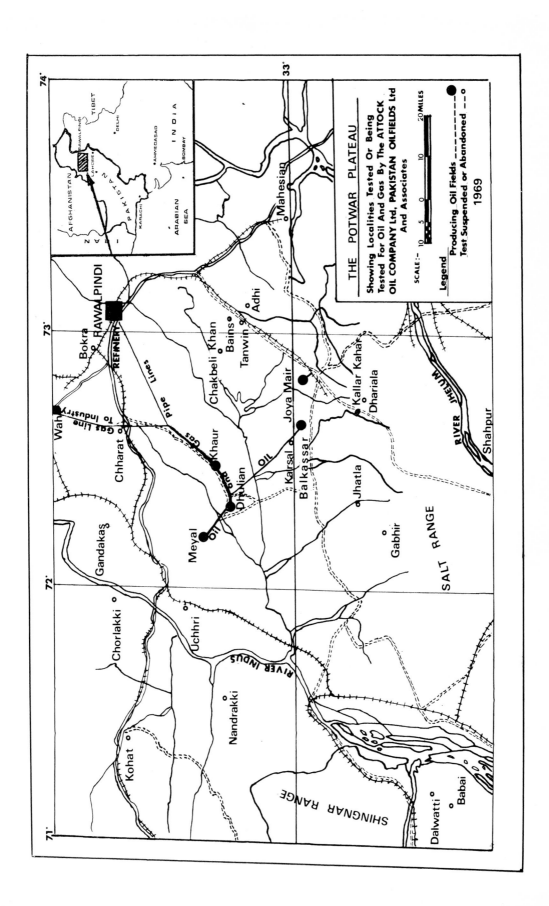

THE POTWAR PLATEAU

Showing Localities Tested Or Being
Tested For Oil And Gas By The ATTOCK
OIL COMPANY Ltd, PAKISTAN OILFIELDS Ltd
And Associates

SCALE:– 10 5 0   5   10   20 MILES

Legend

● Producing Oil Fields ---
○ Test Suspended or Abandoned --○--

1969

In our present age of 'built-in obsolescence' here is a telling reminder of man's capacity for craftsmanship; and, where Rendall's modesty restrained, let us praise now the ship's engineers who for over forty years kept those spare tubes in their racks.

Shwedagon is gone; but what a sounding of sirens there must have been when her ghostly outlines crossed the ultimate bar! Her bell reposes honourably in Steels' head office at Dorking today.

* * *

From the Burma scene we leapfrog nearly 2,000 miles across India (or follow the wake of *Shwedagon* on one of her infrequent voyages to Karachi) into what in 1947 became Pakistan. Here, since their first discovery in 1915, The Attock Oil Company has filled the role of the country's principal producer of petroleum.

The Attock story has been extensively told by writers from its administrative, geological and refining staffs; and in 1963 the Company produced *Golden Jubilee*, a record of the first fifty years since its incorporation. It also sponsors its own quarterly House magazine, so the independent chronicler risks verbal indigestion in any attempt at a succinct review.

The first serious attempts to drill for oil in what is now Pakistan were made in 1887–1890. The deepest penetration achieved was about 750 feet, a remarkable performance for the equipment of the day. Limited success was achieved in that some locally produced oil was used as fuel on the Quetta railway, while the long-defunct Rawalpindi Gas Company used oil in small quantity for over twenty years. In the absence of any significant discovery, however, the pioneers had mostly disappeared by the end of the nineteenth century.

Early in the present century, such small-scale efforts at prospecting as were continuing received encouragement from the then Lieutenant-Governor of the Punjab, the late Sir Louis W. Dane, G.C.I.E., C.S.I. The nearest known workable oil was in Assam, 1,300 miles away, yet Sir Louis, a pioneer at heart, campaigned for more prospecting and drilling in the Punjab.

It was in these unpromising circumstances that the aid of Steels was sought by a small syndicate that had been formed, mainly as a result of the Lieutenant-Governors' urgings, by the late Mr. Frank J. Mitchell (whose other claim to fame it was that he first put trout into the rivers of Kashmir). Steels by this time had had some years of stimulating experience at Yenangyaung, as already described, but production there was now declining and the call of 'wildcatting' was strong. Together with Mr. Mitchell and a few of his friends, they incorporated The Attock Oil Company on 1st December 1913, the name being taken from the District in which Mr. Mitchell had taken out his leases. Steels were appointed Managing Agents and promptly seconded to the infant company one of their Burma geologists, Ernest Shepherd Pinfold (1910–1969), who subsequently was to earn a considerable reputation in his profession. Sir Louis Dane, after retirement from gubernatorial service, appropriately joined the Attock Board in 1914 and was Chairman of the Company from 1930 to 1943.

One is tempted, *en passant*, to compare the role of the two Knights, Abdul Jamal and Louis Dane. They probably had little in common beyond that they both spurred Steels into the way that they should go.

Pinfold started by examining the areas already held under licence by Mitchell. He found that these had been applied for only to cover seepages and that prospects of workable oil were poor. Accordingly a search was made for structures having sufficient size and 'closure' to make possible the entrapment of oil in quantity. Prospecting in the Punjab of those days was not a matter of smooth travel along *pucca* roads (though one day it was to be Attock bitumen that surfaced Pinfold's tracks). Nor was the ubiquitous jeep available for cross-country exploration. Horse, camel and foot were the prospector's choice of conveyance. Nevertheless it was only a short time before Pinfold was able to recommend drilling on a structure named Khaur after a nearby village. The location was some 30 miles south of Mitchell's original leases and about 50 miles from Rawalpindi.

No time was lost. The drilling equipment was provided by I.B.P., two drillers were engaged in the U.S.A., and a member of Steels' Burma staff was transferred to Khaur to take administrative charge of the venture. Drilling started on 22nd January 1915, and at the very shallow depth of 223 feet—the conditions being astonishingly reminiscent of Yenangyaung—the well struck oil.

This was the first of some hundreds of wells drilled at Khaur over the next forty years. They drew their oil from 'pockets' of varying depth or, only yards away from good producers, were bone-dry. They encountered high pressures at about 5,000 feet not previously experienced in the world-wide history of drilling. They claimed lives by fire and blow-out. In 1970, the discovery well, having been deepened progressively to 4,240 feet, was still producing a few gallons of oil daily.

Khaur gave Attock its glamour and romance, and the tales of anxiety and hazard that soon there will be none left to tell. It also attracted a measure of international renown. A young geologist engaged by Attock in the nineteen fifties was surprised to find that Khaur was one of the company's oilfields. He was familiar with it as a 'set piece' at his School of Mines. But Khaur proved to be a very fickle mistress, and it was not until years later, when bigger prizes were won at Dhulian, Joya Mair, Balkassar and Meyal, that Attock's status was firmly established. Extracts from production statistics well illustrate the see-saw approach to ultimate success—

1915–21	23,372	barrels
1922	192,904	,,
1934	85,133	,,
1941	869,672	,,
1946	295,293	,,
1950	659,769	,,
1960	1,859,867	,,
1970	2,774,061	,,

From 1950 onwards, the spectacular increase in production was mainly derived from deeper horizons at Dhulian which, though for long a matter of speculation, had not been tested during the earlier years reckoned palmy after the frustrations and disappointments of Khaur. The spur finally to drill deeper came from the encroachment of water into the upper horizon, causing a decline in oil production that nothing could arrest. Progressively, at two deeper geological horizons, oil was proved in substantial quantity and, in association with it, a volume of gas far beyond the needs of internal consumption or of any case for burning it to waste.

So it was, in 1955, that a gas line from Dhulian to Rawalpindi was bedded down alongside the oil lines. Not long afterwards gas was meeting the fuel needs of the Refinery, the Rawalpindi Electric Power Company, Ordnance and Cement factories, brick kilns and other consumers.

For the Refinery at Morgah, near Rawalpindi, the problems created by an unpredictable production performance were many and varied; and for many years Morgah limped along on little better than a starvation diet of Khaur crude. The strike at Dhulian in 1937 provided a desperately needed boost and, since there was no fundamental difference in quality between the Khaur and Dhulian crudes, no refining problems were raised, though there were costly purchases of new plant to handle the prospective increase in total production.

The strike at Joya Mair in 1944 introduced an astonishing complication. The jet-black crude was so viscous that, in cold weather, you could lob a brick into an open tankfull of the stuff and the brick just sat there—on the surface. There was no pipe-line pumping of crude like this. The only practicable solution was transport by rail, to which end a siding was run out from the nearest railway station to a heating and transfer plant erected about three miles from the field. To this plant Joya Mair crude flows direct from the well-head before it has time to cool and congeal. From the plant, after being steam-heated back to mobility, it is pumped into tank wagons and railed to the Refinery. There it is again necessary to steam-heat the crude before it can be decanted and pumped to the processing plant. Nevertheless, and despite its role as the Refinery's 'problem child', the refined and treated Joya Mair crude provides the base for the excellent bitumen with which thousands of miles of Pakistan's roads are surfaced.

The strike at Balkassar in 1946 introduced into the Refinery equation yet another quality of crude. Like Joya Mair it had a bitumen base but, fortunately, lighter components gave it a fluidity that made it possible to pump it over sixty miles to the Refinery as soon as a pipeline to Khaur had been laid. However, until 1960, the section of the pipeline from Khaur to the Refinery was the common carrier for both the green crudes of Khaur and Dhulian and the black of Balkassar. The two were too dissimilar to be mixed, and so were pumped to the Refinery in batches—so many days of green alternating with so many days of black. This called for additional tankage at the Fields so that one crude could be accumulated in stock while the other was on the move. In 1960 a second oil line was laid from Khaur to the Refinery. Thereafter both crudes have been pumped simultaneously instead of in sequence—a much more satisfactory arrangement.

The Meyal structure geologically was something of a 'Siamese twin' to Dhulian and, therefore, an obvious target for the prospector. For nearly fifty years, however, starting with abortive attempts by the Burmah Oil Company, oil eluded the drill. Attock's deepest well, after the B.O.C. had relinquished, was dry to 10,501 feet (the American driller in charge having some superstition about abandoning at a round 10,500 feet as ordered). Success finally came in 1968

71

when Attock's Pakistani subsidiary, Pakistan Oilfields Limited, struck oil in substantial quantity and of a quality fairly comparable with that of Dhulian, at a depth of about 12,500 feet.

At the Morgah Refinery the original distillation units, designed for a through-put of 2,500 barrels daily, were added to when the Dhulian Field was discovered in 1937. To meet increasing production in more recent years, further adaptations have been made and the Refinery continues to handle all the crude which is produced despite the greatly varying qualities. It has also 'taken in' oil produced by a B.O.C. subsidiary which shares the Balkassar structure with Attock, and the production obtained for a Pakistan Government Agency by drillers and equipment brought in from the Soviet Union.

So it is that a Refinery, designed no more than to process a specific quality of crude, has of recurring necessity been adapted to the point where it can be claimed now that there are few refineries in the world processing such a wide range of petroleum products—from jet fuel to road bitumen, candle wax to diesel oil, lubricants to cleaning fluid, motor spirit to furnace oil. The long trains of railway wagons daily to be seen entering the Refinery filling and marshalling yard are testimony to the resolution and foresight that carried Attock through the dark days in the history of Khaur, as well as to the versatility and improvisation that have adapted the Refinery to meet the unexpected calls that have been made upon it from time to time.

Before leaving this story of oil, and its problems and disappointments, it would be wrong to say nothing at all about the flesh and blood that produces and processes it. The Attock scene typifies, Steels-wide, a consideration which, had it been lacking, would never have yielded the goodwill and the friendships to which all can lay claim. For this purpose we borrow from *Golden Jubilee*—

> What now of the human side of the story? What of the men who drill the wells, operate refining plant, work in laboratories, man the essential services and stand guard over valuable equipment? There are over four thousand of them, widely scattered and variously employed. Nevertheless they are a well-organised body of men who many years ago formed their own Union to speak for them . . . on matters affecting their day-to-day welfare. The benefits accrue to both sides, and the Labour are essentially loyal and proud of their vocations.
>
> A senior staff that pre-war was composed wholly of Britons and Americans is now over two-thirds Pakistani—a proportion that increases yearly. Most of the Pakistanis joined the Company young and have learned their skills as members of its staff. Very few of them leave once they are established. Some are already in positions of con-siderable responsibility.

[In the last few months of the hundred years that go to make this story, Tausif Lodhi, who joined Steels in 1947 on release from war-time naval service, became Attock's first Pakistani General Manager. By that time, also, the British staff had shrunk to a mere handful.]

> As regards the much larger body of workers, their living conditions, their amenities and expectations, the best means of introduction, perhaps, will be to take the reader on an aerial survey in the Company's aircraft.
>
> We take off from a strip which crosses the Company's Morgah golf course and bank over the Refinery and the residential area. Being the lunch break, we can see the queue outside the Refinery canteen, where the day-shift workers can obtain hot meals at subsidized rates. Outside the Refinery walls we can see the Hospital, which has in-

patient accommodation for both men and women. (The Company employs a staff of well-qualified Doctors, including Lady-Doctors for the wives and female dependents of the staff). Not far away is the Workers' Club overlooking the hockey pitch whereon 'The Attock Reds' developed the mastery and co-ordination that have made them nationally famous and earned for their captain an Olympic gold medal. The Senior Staff club, with its tennis courts and swimming pool, is also visible.

Banking again, we cross the sports field, the Millar park, the ration stand (selling subsidized flour and sugar), the orderly rows of Labour quarters (lighting and running water installed) and the Elliott High School. Thence we head for open country and the twenty minutes flight to Khaur. As we approach, see how clearly we can recognize from the air the geologically closed structure that Pinfold had to decipher on foot fifty years ago.

For all its reduced status as an oilfield, Khaur is still the Fields headquarters. Hence the seeming proliferation of clubs, tennis courts, sports ground, hospital and schools. . . . There are film shows in Khaur every week, one in English and one in Urdu.

It is not your imagination deceiving you if the villages around Khaur and Dhulian seem to display an above-average prosperity. For half a century their menfolk have been contributing to and benefiting from the growth of Attock's fortunes. They are men who at the end of their service have taken home with them—from Provident Fund and Gratuity scheme—capital savings undreamt of by the mass of their fellow-countrymen. Their talents too they took with them, using them domestically to raise the standard of village living: and memories of fair, impartial treatment also are theirs. Their sons work for the Company and their grandchildren go to schools that are within sight or sound of the derricks. Attock has rewarded well the labour she has called on.

*   *   *

Before taking leave of Attock, it is necesary that we look at a significant role shared by Attock and I.B.P. during the immediate post-war years.

It was a period during which no phoenix had yet risen from the ashes of Burma. Indeed, preliminary ventures in Canada were not faring well, and there was little to show elsewhere for an unfamiliar questing after diversification. It was an era—in the nineteen fifties—when the two oil companies virtually kept Steels going; Attock by the discovery of new oilfields, as already described; I.B.P. by resolute maintenance of a marketing role no longer fortified by command of its own source of supply.

After the Japanese occupation of Burma, the Government of India introduced legislation enabling refugee bodies corporate to take out temporary registration in India. This legislation carried the option of permanent registration. I.B.P., guided by the writing on the wall, successively took advantage of both opportunities.

The unopposed activities of a Japanese naval squadron marauding along the coasts of the Bay of Bengal early determined the stripping of I.B.P.'s Chittagong installation and the removal of the best of the equipment to Calcutta. Thence it never returned to Chittagong. A post-war arrangement with the Burmah Oil Company for the joint operation of a modernised import and distribution terminal at Chittagong rendered the plant redundant in that context.

The war that destroyed I.B.P. in Burma paradoxically granted a reprieve in India. It was no time for weeding out any organisation, no matter how small, that was staffed, equipped and experienced to market petroleum products within the sub-continent. With the gratefully acknowledged backing of the Burmah Oil Company, I.B.P. became a part of the network that both rationed and distributed oil supplies drawn from whatsoever source could provide—mostly Middle East countries.

The end of the war in 1945 might have been expected to terminate the emergency measures that had kept I.B.P. afloat, but, in 1947, came the sanguinary events that resulted in the fission of the sub-continent into a truncated India flanked by the two enclaves of the newly-born and hostile Pakistan. This raised new and unimagined marketing complications and, for I.B.P., the virtual loss of Chittagong as a contributor to the company's fortunes. Located as it was, a limb of an Indian corporation on Pakistani soil, its profits henceforward were frozen.

Because of this new and ghastly round of tragedy, the special war-time supply arrangement persisted into the nineteen fifties. By that time the challenge of American oil companies in a land where the British writ no longer ran was vigorous. In the circumstances the small but closely controlled organisation that was I.B.P. was an ally not to be scorned by the Burmah-Shell marketing organisation that for so long had dominated the scene. Throughout a bitterly competitive period, I.B.P. received valuable support from its major partner, for whom much of the oil made available to I.B.P. was sold on consignment.

Survival demanded, however, much capital outlay in modernising service stations, transport and related facilities to match the competition. Calcutta and Bombay traditionally had been I.B.P.'s main bases; but the demands of distance now compelled the establishment of a third branch in Delhi, which carved its marketing area out of the over-stretched spheres of the other two. It was a not-to-be-regretted move; but it cost I.B.P. much to stay in the field.

The Steels-wide compulsion to diversify did not exclude I.B.P. When joint-venture arrangements for the post-war Burma oil industry brought in that country's Government to the initial extent of a one-third stake, I.B.P.'s cash share of the proceeds of disinvestment led to the purchase of a twenty-five per cent share of the equity of Balmer, Laurie & Co. Ltd., a long-established and respected Calcutta industrial and agency house of London parentage. This company's interests ranged over the production, warehousing and marketing of tea; heavy and light engineering; steel fabrication, including a wide range of containers; and the manufacture of switchboard and other electrical equipment. Their sphere of activity was Calcutta and the Assam area.

In Bombay, earlier than elsewhere in India, the post-war manufacture of four-gallon kerosene tins ('the flimsy') ran into decline as the small consumer came to learn that bulk supply was cheaper and that a requirement of less than four gallons was not scorned. In I.B.P.'s closing years, therefore, the Bombay installation's engineering facilities were imaginatively adapted, first to the production of bottle washing equipment, and later to the manufacture of electronic equipment and components, automatic timing devices, relays and 'pacemakers'. The work involved was carried out, very largely, by the staff of erstwhile tin makers, patiently and successfully re-trained.

For political reasons, however, the striving after survival was not to endure; and by 1970 the 'moving finger' had counselled that I.B.P. be sold to Indian interests. Though the company's glamour belongs, perhaps, to the Burma oilfields, the *finale* on Indian soil must be viewed much as one does a rearguard action that gains time vital to successful re-deployment elsewhere.

* * *

To complete Steels' oil story to 1970, space must briefly be found for their efforts to find oil in England. These were sporadic over the period 1937–1968 with, of course, total suspension during the war years of 1939–1945. Progress was keenly followed, particularly by those in intemperate climes who aspired to a transfer as Field Agent, Yorkshire and Derbyshire!

Test wells were drilled at Edale in Derbyshire, and at Croxteth, very near to the Aintree race course in Lancashire. These were followed by a well in Yorkshire drilled in partnership with the Ambassador Oil Company and its associates. The total production from this exploration was a bottle of green crude and some gas from Croxteth, which proved to be a badly fractured structure. It is interesting to speculate, however, what the reactions might have been if commercial oil had been found at Croxteth extending to below Beecher's Brook!

So, in the opening years of Steels' second century, The Attock Oil Company stands as the only surviving testimonial to sixty years' harvesting of skill, experience and success in the glamorous search for oil. An 'ear to the ground', however, is never lacking; and it is to be hoped that an adventurous continuum may yet enrich the material available to the future chronicler.

CHAPTER V

SEA LANES AND WATERWAYS

The Imports and the Shipping Departments in Burma drew their strength from the Rangoon River and the many vessels that entered its muddy waters. The Cotton and Sundry Produce Department would have been as nothing without its domination of the Irrawaddy as it flowed through Burma's dry belt. The Burma Cement Company needed no advertisement beyond those tall, gleaming silos on the river bank at Thayetmyo: and, far to the south of them all, the Lenya Mining Company took its feed from the bed of the Yamone chaung.

Here, then, is a common riverine thread wherewith to bind these disparate activities together for the purpose of this present chapter.

The traditional *boxwallah*, usually a Chinaman, was he who respectfully and unobtrusively presented himself on your verandah on a week-end afternoon. From his head he lowered a balloon-like bundle, which he then opened and dissected for your inspection—silks, jade, lace table cloths and brass ware (which latter, even though it might bear the stamp of Birmingham, had been humped over chilling Asian passes for your delight). Any succeeding transaction was sealed almost as an act of reverence. The word *Chinaman*, alas, is now deemed derogatory. The present writer resurrects it, this last once, because he does not recall it in other than friendly contexts. The term *boxwallah* likewise earned a worthy niche. There were those who bestowed it upon the trader at large as a seal of denigration. It was a case of design frustrated when the latter so often wore it as a compliment. Certainly there will be no cloaking the fact that Steels achieved mastery in the *boxwallah's* role.

In the opening chapter of this story the point was made that Strang Steel's original trading was in piecegoods; and Walter Frames has recorded that in the eighteen-eighties he was "packing cartons (of silk) in Wood Street and the Cutler Street warehouses".

As Steels' involvement in rice and timber and oil grew and prospered, United Kingdom manufacturers and suppliers seeking overseas representation were not slow to recognise that the company was strongly placed to market their wares both within and without their own widening organization. If, for example, Steels in Burma had never sold a case of beer outside the circle of their own staff, friends and associates, it seems unlikely that John Jeffery & Co. Ltd. would have sought other representation, for this 'market' alone covered many thirsts in a climate that could be torrid.

The representational range was enormous as even a minimum sampling will show—

> Acrylics, condensers and dies,
>   Precision tools, jellies and poles,
> Insecticides, oilman's supplies,
>   Brake linings and rubberized soles.
>
> Confectionery, wagons and nails,
>   Belt lacing and tampers and tyres,
> Compressors and piecegoods and rails,
>   Abrasives and copperweld wires.
>
> Refacers and cheeses and chucks,
>   Hoist pulleys and aircraft and meats,
> Enamels and cordage and trucks
>   Extinguishers, varnish and sheets.
>
> Champagne, generators and fans,
>   Appliances, polishes, cars,
> Asbestos, provisions in cans,
>   Domestic ware, cycles, cigars.

In the event that a member of the staff required a mobile mechanical shovel or a gas-fired reverberatory furnace, he would have been in the strong position, of course, of being able to secure it at the 'staff rate'.

In a fast changing world, entrepôt trading is a catch-as-catch-can activity. It must be well-informed and flexible if it is to keep up with developments. Natural disasters, overthrow of regimes, changing fashions, down-grading of natural products by synthetic substitutes—all these and more are factors which can close or open trading prospects.

Steels' imports/exports business in Burma was built on the British manufacturing market, but it never lacked for overseas involvement once extra-Burma branches in Siam, India, Ceylon and elsewhere came to be established. This led frequently to intriguing inter-port business in unheard of commodities, and sometimes to representation in Burma and elsewhere for the foreign companies that marketed them.

Even though it was under the impulse of war, a unique venture, while it lasted, was the opening in 1939 of a branch at Kunming in China's Yunnan Province; a place that might as well have been located on the moon until it became tenuously linked to Lashio in the Northern Shan States by the historic 'Burma Road'.

The establishment of the branch fell to Eric Robert Mackay (1927–1962), whose ultimate record it was during his service with Steels that he opened five trading branches outside of Burma, four in Asia and one in Canada. Mackay's personal memoirs well describe the Kunming story—

> The initiative for this move came from the Chinese National Government then located in Chungking, who wished to encourage trade via the Burma Road, the only remaining route into "Free China"; and had even promised us space for our goods on their trucks operating between Burma and Kunming. In the event, however, no space

was forthcoming and it became evident that if we were to do any trading, we would have to provide our own transport. In 1940, therefore, Steels made a start in Burma Road transport by putting six Dodge trucks into service.

The Burma Road was a remarkable undertaking when one thinks that it was constructed by Chinese labour with little or no mechanical equipment. The route ran from Lashio to Kunming, a distance of some 750 miles, across the Himalaya foothills, surmounting mountain passes of up to 7000 feet and with suspension bridge crossings at the Salween and Mekong rivers. Japanese bombing of the road was frequent but ineffective and casualties were mainly due to road washouts and trucks being lost over the *khud*. Petrol for the return journey to Burma had to be carried in by our convoys and payload was reduced accordingly. However, business prospered and when the Japanese invaded Burma in 1942 we had a fleet of 180 trucks operating on the Burma Road with a large servicing and maintenance establishment in Lashio.

Our principal import into China was cotton yarn for the cottage weaving industry, supplied from Steels' spinning mill at Myingyan and from Indian mills; but the demand was insatiable for all types of goods and we handled enquiries ranging literally from biscuits to locomotives. One interesting project we worked on with the Chinese Government was to improve the surface by laying a double track of concrete the whole length of the Burma Road. In the event the deal did not go through, but I remember figuring the quantities and the cement required would have kept the Burma Cement factory busy for quite a time. Another interesting transaction was when we sold a full cargo of raw cotton from our Bombay office to the local Kunming spinning mill for delivery ex rail Lashio.

Return freight for our trucks in the form of export cargo was not easy to come by owing to difficulties of internal transport in China, but we were able to assemble shipments of such varying China produce as hog bristles, wood oil, raw silk, gall nuts and wolfram. One unusual export enquiry was for silkworm eggs for the Government of Kashmir which we shipped by R.A.F. plane from Kunming to Rawalpindi.

In Kunming, conditions were of course somewhat abnormal and, with a seller's market existing, there was rarely any question of a "hard sell". Rather our problems were in getting the goods to Kunming. There were no telephones and the telegraph line with Burma was frequently down. Japanese bomber raids were a daily occurrence and business had to be conducted where and when one could.

After the war Mackay was sent on a mission of reconnaissance to Hongkong, Shanghai, Canton and Kunming. It is not surprising that straws in the prevailing wind pointed to the first of these as the surest prospect, and the Hongkong branch was established in 1946. Despite that so recently it had been Japanese-occupied, Hongkong staged a remarkably swift return to active trading. The main consuming market was China, and, among other things, Steels imported considerable quantities of textiles to meet the demand. In the reverse direction a brisk trade was done in exporting Hongkong cotton yarn to Steels' branches—Chittagong in particular.

Pre-war experience at Kunming stood Steels in good stead and export business in China produce was soon established—wood oil, teaseed oil, China tea, cassia lignea and ginger, though trading in such commodities became difficult as the Communist Government of China progressively controlled the flow of produce to Hongkong. In an entrepreneurial role, and thanks to overseas branches and connections, direct shipments were arranged such as cotton yarn from Italy and Egypt to East Pakistan and Burma, raw cotton from West Pakistan to North China, sugar from Taiwan to Japan and gunny bags from Calcutta to Shanghai.

By the mid 1950s the increasing grip of Communism in China was making for trading difficulties and uncertainties, and there was free circulation of wild rumours as the confrontation with the Nationalist rump in Taiwan developed. In 1959 the decision was taken to close the Hongkong office. The subsequent history of the colony suggests that here perhaps was misjudgment.

In 1949 an office was opened in Tokyo, and in 1951 a branch office in Osaka. At that time trade in Japan was being controlled by the occupation administration, but, as this was phased out, a resurgence of Japanese business practices made for discriminatory licensing and taxation procedures aimed at foreign enterprises. Steels did a fair amount of trading with their branches elsewhere in Asia and in the Middle East; but the burden of maintaining an establishment in Japan, where the cost of living then was probably the highest in the world, proved too heavy and the Japanese venture was abandoned in 1959.

Post-war in Burma, Steels' Imports Department re-opened as soon as possible, and very large quantities of piecegoods and other necessities were imported to meet the needs of a devastated country. The department, with its Burma Road experience to fortify the decision, expanded into the transport business, and a large motor workshop was built and equipped at Steels' old East Saw Mill premises at Dunneedaw near Rangoon.

Pre-war, the 'Strand' had been Rangoon's premier hotel. In 1948 Steels purchased the dilapidated shell, re-built it and opened in 1949. Thereafter the 'Strand' offered a high standard of accommodation, was the venue for many Government and private functions and became popular with the Burmese community for wedding receptions. A later venture, in partnership with the Government, was the operation of a holiday hotel at Sandoway on the Arakan coast and a small hotel at Taunggyi in the Shan States.

In the hoped-for brave new world, however, these and other ventures were to prove sterile as the steam roller of State control overrode the prospects for foreign participation in the rehabilitation of Burma. In 1963 the Imports Department in Burma was closed down after over ninety years of trading as just about everybody's friend. First on the scene, it was the last to go.

*   *   *

In the Rice Department's story, J. B. Clark's brief summary of nineteenth century Burmese history has shown with what speed and under what circumstances Rangoon was transformed from a sleepy hollow into a major port. Like the Imports Department, the Shipping Department owed its growth to the standing which Steels acquired in a country that relatively was so late a comer into the community of trading nations. When the time came, the British shipping lines had no need to look beyond the firm which so markedly was playing a leading role in establishing Burma as the rice bowl of the Orient.

A catalogue of names can be tedious, but a selection from the agencies held carries the music of nostalgic familiarity—Bibby and Henderson, Anchor and Brocklebank, British-India, Blue Funnel and Clan, Elder Dempster and Furness, Union Castle and Lamport & Holt. Others, less familiar, flew the flags of India, the U.S.A., Denmark, Norway and Japan, while others yet, casual callers at Burma ports where they had no representation, were frequently directed to Steels' care. A surprising plant at the bottom of the garden was the U.S.S.R. line owned by V/O Sovracht of Moscow.

It all added up to an imposing charge. It conferred advantages, of course, in such matters as securing priority of space for a last-minute rice export order or an inward consignment of urgently-needed oilfield equipment. It could also produce, at short notice, that badly-needed cabin accommodation in a fully-booked ship. These, however, were the reasonable privileges of solid service which, in its turn, bred friendships between ship and shore that had a habit of enduring despite that they were renewable only at irregular intervals.

As a related activity to shipping, the Insurance Department in Rangoon acted as Principal Agents, underwriting all types of insurance on behalf of nine British companies—The Royal, Atlas, Queensland, Motor Union, Alliance, Law Union & Rock, Northern, Union of Canton and North British & Mercantile. Some of these agency appointments dated from late in the nineteenth century. In 1920, by the takeover of George Gordon & Co., Steels inherited the appointment of Lloyds Agents in Rangoon, which the former company had held since 1893. In this capacity they accommodated a staff of Lloyds Surveyors to deal, among other things, with damaged cargoes.

After the Japanese war, until they closed, both the Shipping and Insurance Departments were busy and profitable and had expanded their scope to include airline agencies, particularly for Cathay Airlines and the British Overseas Airways Corporation. Both Departments, very largely, were under the management of Burmese executives who, having been trained pre-war, had re-joined thereafter. Some of these continued to operate on their own account after Steels had departed, but only for the limited period left before Government extended its nationalisation policy to practically all commercial activities.

*   *   *

The manner of Abdul Karim Jamal's involvement with Steels in their venture into oil winning is told elsewhere. The history of The Consolidated Cotton and Oil Mills Limited provides an earlier illustration of this remarkable man's ubiquity.

Preceding by some ten years his own entry into the oil drilling business, Jamal had installed a cotton ginning and baling plant at Myingyan, on the Irrawaddy river not far south of its confluence with the Chindwin. This he followed a year later with a similar installation at Allanmyo some 150 miles down-stream. These two towns span the core of Burma's dry zone and the country's cotton growing acres. They also embrace the Irrawaddy oilfields, wherein lies a clue to Jamal's later diversification from cotton into crude. On passage between his twin establishments, the activity at Yenangyaung, clearly visible from the river, must have caught his imagination and fired his ambition.

A cotton gin is a machine for separating the cotton fibre, known as lint, from the seed; so the addition a year or two later of plant for the milling of the seed itself was a logical progression. However, cotton ginning on the banks of the Irrawaddy was not an activity in which Jamal was an unchallenged pioneer. From the outset he had at least two major competitors to contest his supremacy and strain his finances. In 1907 he formed his business into a limited company and appointed Steels as Managing Agents. His rivals likewise were employing British companies in the same capacity.

An occupational hazard faced by the cotton industry in Burma was the unpredictability of the annual rainfall in the dry zone. A bad year could limit the crop to 75,000 bales; a good year could nearly double the figure. The war years of 1914–1918 provided great incentive to the existing traders to expand and to a rash of small, mostly Indian, newcomers to undertake commitments; but so catastrophic was the slump that followed the war that nearly all went under, some being bought out by Jamals until they, Jamals, were the only significant survivor. Then the Jamal family, in the hope of riding out the cotton slump, embarked on speculative dealings in the rice market. So disastrous were the results that they were forced to put their cotton business into liquidation. It was taken over by Steels, to be run thenceforward as the mainstay of what became the Cotton and Sundry Produce Department.

This department came to control some sixty per cent of Burma's cotton crop. About a fifth of the lint was converted into yarn at the company's spinning mills. The balance was exported unspun. A total of about 25,000 tons of cottonseed was milled annually, of which about seventy per cent was refined as cottonseed oil, the base for soap, while the remainder, the non-oily residue, was marketed as cattle cake.

As a parallel operation to the milling of the cottonseed, some 40,000 tons of groundnuts were milled annually to provide oil and cake for similar purposes. With it all there was trading in white beans, cutch and maize—a total operation that employed some 3000 people, mostly Burmans.

After the Second World war, the installations at Myingyan and Allanmyo were re-built but, in the ensuing upheaval, were again damaged or destroyed, and for considerable periods were in the hands of insurgents. This spelt the end for The Consolidated Cotton and Oil Mills, though in Rangoon the Cotton and Sundry Produce Department continued to purchase cotton, beans and oilcake from other producers. With the help of their old brokers and connections in the business, the department was able to control quality and to export large quantities of these commodities until such business was taken over by the Government.

So it was with Steels' rubber estate at Hlawga near Rangoon. This and other small estates had been acquired just before the war. The trees survived hostilities and, through the Cotton and Sundry Produce Department, good quality rubber was produced and exported until the same fate befell.

*   *   *

The story of the Burma Cement Company, paradoxically, has its beginnings in an unsuccessful attempt to find oil.

Nine miles westward of Thayetmyo on the Irrawaddy, and some sixty miles south of the riches of Yenangyaung on the opposite bank, was a jungle-covered, geologically domed structure known as Pyaye. For some time, in the same general area, oil had been produced in small quantities from shallow depths by a private, family enterprise; but, for reasons that would be overridden today, the greater prospects of the area had been rated low by the contemporary Burma geologists. Pyaye, accordingly, slumbered and slept while other leases, deemed more attractive, were being tested.

In 1935, the Indo-Burma Petroleum Company started drilling a cable tools test well at Pyaye (i.e. a well drilled by the percussion method, possibly nowhere now to be seen). Several low-pressure gas sands were encountered in the first thousand feet. Their combined capacity was such as to justify the sinking of a few shallow wells to harness this gas as fuel for deeper drilling. At about 1600 feet the exploration well struck high-pressure gas but, with the hole kept full of water, it was found possible to continue. At around 2500 feet the drill entered another high-pressure sand, and this time there was no holding it. The combined

81

effect of the two pressure zones was to cause a violent outburst that blew the drilling tools out of the hole. Control of the well was lost, and was to remain lost for several months while special high-pressure equipment feverishly was sought and obtained from the U.S.A.

During this paralysing period the well blew wild: the flow was estimated at about twenty million cubic feet of gas daily: the roar of the escape could be heard by travellers on the Irrawaddy: verbal communication within some hundreds of yards of the well was impossible, and instructions from drillers to their gangs had to be given and received at the bottom of a deep *chaung* where they could be heard. Nothing like this had happened in Burma before.

Once the American equipment arrived, the well was successfully brought under control and closed in. Quiet returned to the jungle, but what was to be done with the tamed monster?

Three miles from Thayetmyo, near the track to Pyaye, a knife-edged ridge, the Tondaung hill, rose sharply some 750 feet above the surrounding countryside. Its strata included bands of limestone separated by clay. Sand and water were the abundant contribution of the nearby Irrawaddy and, given cheap fuel, only gypsum immediately was lacking from the formula for cement making. The superfluous, voluminous gas of Pyaye was the magnet that removed all doubts.

The project was launched. Quarries were opened at three points along the Tondaung. They were linked by railed tracks to a central despatch station whence the limestone boulders descended in buckets on a gravity ropeway to the foot of the hill. Hence a metre-gauge locomotive hauled the limestone in wagons from the discharge hopper to the plant on the bank of the Irrawaddy. The gas flowed through an eight inch line from Pyaye and initial consumption was established at about two million cubic feet daily. Gypsum, to start with, was imported from Red Sea quarries; but, once the need for it had been noised abroad, it was not long before the entire requirement was being met from indigenous sources located and worked by Burmese contractors.

The cement making process, in brief terms, comprised an initial grinding to slurry of the limestone in association with calculated proportions of clay, sand and water. The slurry was pumped to the higher end of a sloping and slowly revolving kiln, some two hundred feet long by six feet diameter. The kiln was fired from its lower end, so the slurry was encountering a rising temperature as it made its sluggish way downhill. In sequence, the slurry became dried, calcined and sintered. The final clinker, like small cinders, was cooled and re-ground in a second milling process until, as the finished product, it was blown by air current to the storage silos on the river bank. Thence it was packed in paper bags and sent off by barge to market. A not inconsiderable market it proved to be—expanding from 25,000 tons annually in 1937 to 65,000 tons, the designed capacity of the plant, in the few years that remained before the war.

The opening ceremony, early in 1937, was performed by General Sir Aylmer Hunter-Weston, who was accompanied by his Lady, the daughter of William Strang Steel. It was a memorable occasion, being only the second whereat a cement kiln had been fired *de novo* on natural gas. The imponderables were such as to warrant the flying out from Denmark of two experts. All went without a hitch, and the guests departed each with a miniature cement keg cast from the

The ropeway at Thayetmyo

Cement plant viewed from the Irrawaddy at Thayetmyo

The Tin Dredge at Yamone

The Manager's bungalow, Yamone

first production. They were intended to serve as paper weights: can it be that any of these souvenirs survive?

The staff accommodation at this stage was primitive to those who had been nurtured under oilfield conditions—and most had been transferred thence. The rented quarters lacked electricity and sanitation and were well placed to miss nothing of the noise and aroma of the bazaar. In due course this deficiency reached the top of the priority list, and easy living in the attractive river setting that was Thayetmyo became the norm.

The end for B.C.C. came in the sickeningly familiar mantle of the self-destroyer; for although, after the war, a near-total job of reconstruction was done at Thayetmyo, the company's nationalisation was decreed in 1954 at a time when Steels were actually negotiating to sell a share in the project to Government. In 1959 the Supreme Court upset the nationalisation award and compensation was paid. However, the lights had gone out for those whose dream-turned-reality the cement undertaking had been.

* * *

James Ingram Milne was a hard-bitten Aberdonian with a degree in engineering. For years he had prospected for and worked small-scale tin leases in the Tavoy area of the Tenasserim Archipelago, and in due course he established first one, and then another, sizeable tin-bearing prospect. Both, however, were dredging propositions beyond his financial means, and it was to Steels that he came in quest of a joint venture.

Against this background, in 1938, came to be floated The Lenya Mining Company, with Steels as Managing Agents and Milne as a Director, and as Mine Manager for such period as would be found necessary to train a member of Steels' staff for the job.

The leased properties were known as Yamone and Khe chaung. The latter, the bigger but much the less accessible, receives no further mention because the Japanese invasion terminated the venture before ever operations were extended that far. Certain it is that it remains undredged to this day. Yamone was a riverine prospect near the headwaters of a tidal *chaung* of that name. The annual rainfall exceeded two hundred inches.

The tin bed, covered by some thirty to forty feet of overburden, underlay the river itself and an area of mangrove swamp extending some hundreds of yards back from one bank of the river. An island of rising, non-alluvial ground occupied the opposite bank and, when cleared of thick jungle, accommodated the 'camp'—bungalows and quarters, office, stores godown and tin washing sheds. The workshop was housed aboard the dredge which was a modern, bucket-type vessel of about two hundred feet in length with a uniform beam of about fifty feet. It was crewed mainly by Straits Chinese. Flotation on the river, of course, was no problem; but the dredge was water-borne in a 'paddock' of its own digging as it traversed into the swampy area, pre-cleared of mangrove jungle.

The dredge was built in Holland, dismantled for shipment to Burma, re-erected in the harbour at Mergui and towed through a difficult sea and river passage to the mine. It was powered by vertical suction gas engines fuelled on locally burnt charcoal. The quantity of charcoal required for continuous running was such that a mangrove burning industry had to be created and fostered over an extensive area of waterways, on the banks of which villages were few and far between and very primitive. The coastal swamp, extending deep inland down a very long shore line, knew no roads and therefore no wheels. There were none of the familiar pagodas, *phongyi chaungs* or bazaars. Communication, such as it was, was by dug-out canoe; and literacy was far below the Burma average. Introduction of a cottage industry such as charcoal burning was a daunting, up-hill task in these conditions.

In Mergui itself, the town's proximity to Thailand and Malaya gave it a cosmopolitan veneer not to be matched elsewhere in rural Burma. Maurice Collis's 'Siamese White' was for many people an introduction to an unsuspected corner of the globe, which even the old *Sir Harvey Adamson*, despite her weekly round-trip from Rangoon, did nothing to unfold, for it cannot be recalled that she ever carried a self-confessed tourist; and certainly Mergui's hostelry must have dampened the enthusiasm of any who may have ventured the journey.

It was a beachcomber's coast. If you were a smuggler, here was your risk-free paradise: if a poacher, you were likely to find yourself out-pointed by the Chinese marauders who had denuded the slopes of the Bilauktaung range of the rhinoceros, so keenly hunted for the allegedly aphrodisiac component of its horn. Perhaps these were the ultimate waters where piracy flourished.

The coast was a place of unbelievable beauty, the sea studded with islands, some of them rising sharply through three thousand feet of jungle mantling. The waters of the rivers that riddled the mangrove swamp were intensely fluorescent; and launch travel by night under a full moon, with the phantom, creamy bow wave—and maybe the gleaming plunge of a startled crocodile—challenging the flickering of the millions of fireflies that thronged the banks, was an experience that defies living description. The coast line, in places where it occurred as *terra firma* among the swamp, was often a series of crescent-shaped sandy beaches overhung with shade above the tide line. They were about two hundred yards from horn to horn and totally secluded, the one from its neighbour. To a millionaire, in a location of his own choosing, such a beach would be sold by the sand grain.

Back at the dredge, however, there was trouble. The charcoal burnt from mangrove wood had an exceptionally high calorific value, but it also held in stubborn suspension a tarry substance that packed on top of, and totally inhibited, the vertically-pistoned engines. Horizontal pistons probably would have expelled the tarry particles, but the problem had never been envisaged, and there was certainly no practicable alternative to mangrove as fuel. At intervals of about two days the dredge engines had to be stripped and cleaned on a scale that would have been acceptable every three months. Milne was almost crazed with dis-appointment and frustration. He visited each of the few dredges operating along the coast in search of inspiration, and harried all available expertise in Rangoon before accepting that the Dutch designers must be asked to put in hand with all speed the design and fabrication of special tar extractors. This they did and, after months of delay, the extractors arrived, were installed and did all that was required of them. Soon the dredge was producing between thirty and forty tons of washed tin a month where eleven tons was the minimum needed for profitable working. At least it was demonstrated that the venture was viable.

By this time, however, Hitler was planting the pug marks of Nazi-ism across Europe; and when Japan entered the war, the dredge, with ghastly predictability, was scuttled where she dug.

After the war, Milne, with all his old, stubborn Scottish enthusiasm—and now in his sixties—set out to salvage and refloat the rusting hulk. It was probably a forlorn enterprise in any case, but all hope died when he himself was dacoited and murdered in mid-river while escorting cash from Mergui. Ultimately the dredge was sold for scrap, and what might well have succeeded as a very profitable venture became instead one that were better had it never been born.

* * *

The watery thread that has bound this chapter so far must needs be broken if the story of Steels' mining activities in Burma is to be read as a whole. The setting now becomes the Southern Shan States, perhaps one of Nature's most beautiful countrysides.

The mining involvement started as far back as the war of 1914–1918 when the Timber Department, in the role of middleman, commenced shipping tin and wolfram concentrates to the United Kingdom on a consignment basis. The business, in this form, became unattractive after the war because of the speedier cash settlement that became available by direct selling to the local Mawchi Mines or to smelters in Penang. Prices remained high, however, and detailed geological prospecting was carried out by the Oil Department in the late thirties in the hope of becoming miners instead of middlemen. Some promising wolfram outcrops were tested, but the concentrate value was not high enough for profitable working.

The most successful venture lay in the procurement and shipment of lead slags, wherein Steels' role was that of Lazarus to a Chinese Dives. Many centuries earlier the Chinese had mined and smelted ore in the hills to the north of Heho. The spur to their activity had been the silver content, for the slag, rich in lead, had been rejected. Whether this prodigality was of intent or because of inadequate smelting methods is questionable, because the Chinese technique is not known for certain.

Possibly the method employed by the Shans in recent years, on a much smaller scale, provides some clue to the Chinese technology. The air for their home-made smelters was provided by pumps made of large diameter sections of bamboo installed vertically as a battery. The pistons were smaller bamboos, with feathers secured to the base, which fitted snugly into the larger bamboos. The motive power was supplied by Shan girls standing on a platform of sufficient height to give the optimum stroke. As a delectable prospect the effect was marred by the cloud of sulphur fumes that shrouded the operation. The health hazard was obvious.

The lead content of the Chinese slag averaged 30 to 35 and could be as high as 45 per cent. When washed, the slags were in pellet form resembling marbles: the brighter their glaze, the higher the lead content. The slags were not found in heaps above ground but in subterranean pockets variously from about one to six feet down. Most pockets were located in cultivated plains and valleys, though some were found on hill sides.

With the advent of the Second World War, the tempo of activity increased to the point where the Government of the Shan States itself climbed onto the bandwagon by declaring the slag pockets to be mineral deposits and, therefore, State property—only to be worked after Prospecting Licences to explore and Mining Leases to operate had been applied for and granted. This raised obvious problems of what areas to apply for in the absence of geological rules remotely relevant to slag location. The formula devised by Steels' geologists was unique technically and masterly in its simplicity. The fields were observed while under crops. Where there were bare or thin patches not attributable to surface causes, Licences were applied for.

Activity, by all and sundry, became intense and, by the time war came to Burma, shipments from Rangoon were averaging about a thousand tons per vessel, and accumulations of slag in the field were substantial. On this high note the venture ended.

CHAPTER VI

THE INDIAN OCEAN

This loosely described chapter covers 'outliers', to visit all of which in a single tour by sea would involve many miles of travel in Indian Ocean waters.

Steels' emergence as an established force in Assam before the Japanese war had ended has had some explanation in the opening chapter of this story. After the passing of the emergency—the appalling famine—which brought the establishment into being, Steels were asked and undertook to represent the interests of the Assam Branch of the Indian Tea Association and the other members of the Planting & Commerce Group. It is the case in Assam that the Lower Assam Valley is surplus in rice while an area embracing some three hundred tea-gardens in the Upper Valley is in deficit. Steels' task lay in taking delivery from the rice mills in Lower Assam, this including checking of quality and weight, and arranging despatch to the gardens in Upper Assam and the financial formalities involved.

It sounds pedestrian stuff, but it is evident that something in the way of expertise did not come amiss. An Assam manager, writing in 1950, records that "Much rancour has been raised on the subject of maximum permissible moisture content in Rice. Twelve per cent is safe and thirteen per cent is not. Assam is a sub-montane province and showers in December and January are not infrequent. February is the month of mist. There are too many rice mills and consequently too much competition for paddy so that the cultivators have no need to wait for their grain to dry out before bringing it to market. During the months of January and February the question of damp rice is a constant nightmare. One morning I found a telegram on my desk saying—'Wagon No. XYZ arrived. Clouds of steam emerging. Come quick.' A young assistant whom we had on that month's Assam staff proceeded to Sagamya and solved the immediate difficulty by suggesting the opening of the doors to let the cool breeze in." The identity of this sound thinker, alas, is not on record. One hopes that he went far.

Steamy rice was at least a predictable hazard. Not so was the earthquake of 1950, which extensively damaged buildings, roads and railways and raised stern problems of food distribution. A more insidious consequence, not fully appreciated until 1954, was the tilting of the bed of the Brahmaputra river. In that later year heavy flooding led to violent erosion of the banks where the river sought to change its course. A typical casualty was the Protestant Church at Dibrugarh which, having stood for 110 years some four hundred yards from the river, was swept into oblivion as the ground it stood on was clawed away. In 1957 a series of cyclones extensively disrupted communications and power supply lines. In 1962 there were more floods, wreaking enormous and widespread destruction and failing by only a few inches of further rise to destroy the entire town of Dibrugarh. In 1963 Chinese forces invaded north-east India and advanced so far south that all tea gardens north of the Brahmaputra were evacuated. South of the river, as can be imagined, life was bedevilled by a massive refugee problem at a time when Chinese intentions in regard to a further advance were quite unknown. Rice availability, meanwhile, was parlous in the extreme by reason of the destruction wrought by the previous year's floods. Yet somehow, on the fairest basis possible under unimaginable conditions, rice distribution was effected.

These, in quick parade, are the highlights of the conditions under which Steels procured and distributed rice in Assam for twenty-five years, ended in 1968 by nationalistic decree. Let us hope for their successors in the business an easier row to hoe.

There was another activity in Assam to be recorded. The Lancashire firm of Pilkington Brothers, internationally known as glass makers, acquired rights in 1949, in a remote area in the Khasi and Jaintia Hills, to extract sillimanite, a valuable refractory medium of exceptional density providing an effective insulation for the lining of glass tanks, blast furnaces, etc. Steels purchased a shareholding and were appointed Managing Agents. The project was viable, but difficulties over export licensing put an end to operations after seven years and the business was sold to Indian interests. Steels will be remembered in Assam for a long time to come, but it will be *in absentia*.

*   *   *

Steels opened their Ceylon office at Colombo in 1933. The island today is Sri Lanka, but the earlier name held good for Steels' first century.

The prompting for the move came from the financial failure of the company employed until then as the agent in the island for the Timber and Rice departments. The reaction, however, was less than warm. Typically, the Rice manager of a Colombo firm is quoted as saying—"We do not appreciate Steels' presence here. This we know is the thin end of the wedge and they will endeavour to spread their tentacles over our rubber and tea business. We are quite satisfied with the arrangements we have for importing through native dealers and we are not inclined to cut them out for you." It is not without interest that the company for which this man spoke appears in the list of those whose rice requirements, in whole or part, ultimately were procured through Steels.

Opposition on the tea and coffee estates from managers of ingrained habits or from foremen with something in it for themselves was to be expected. There seems also to have been some anti-Burma prejudice in other circles. In 1947, for example, in a context other than that of rice, a Government Press notice declared that—"It has now been definitely established that the cases of poisoning reported were caused by the eating of a large quantity of one or other of the following beans—Rangoon Red Beans, Rangoon White Beans, Rangoon Sultan Beans". To this black charge the Colombo manager of the day vigorously riposted

—"The extraordinary thing is that folk here who have lived in Burma appear to be immune and have had excellent meals from samples of the deadly beans drawn from Government stores . . .".

So far as rice in Ceylon is concerned, the selling point that seems finally to have won the day was the quality of Steels' rice, which was parboiled and stored for a week or two before shipment so as to give it a locally-popular dusty appearance. There was the attendant advantage, where coolie labour practice was to cook the morrow's rice overnight, that parboiled rice is slower to sour after cooking than straight-milled grain. Add that a practice of bagging to $2\frac{1}{2}$ pounds overweight resulted in outturn losses wholly acceptable by comparison with previous experience, and it will be understood that even the hard of heart among estate managers were softened progressively.

Another, and recurrent, Colombo hazard was posed by the frequent arrival in port of a Rangoon-bound Bibby or Henderson liner. On board there was likely to be either a manager's wife looking for V.I.P. treatment, or a fiancée for whom special chaperonage had been requested at this last port of call before the Church door, or a despairing mother floored by the discovery that the reserve nappies had gone into the hold instead of the baggage room, or a bachelor assistant looking for a party of the Colombo manager's contriving. The said manager's office—indeed his very desk—commanded a view of the harbour entrance, so he could see what was coming to him.

The import-export business of E. B. Creasy & Company was acquired by Steels in 1951 after a first interest had been taken three years earlier. The then chairman was the third E. B. Creasy successively to occupy the position, a remarkable record. His founding grandfather was of the adventurous generation whence the Victorian era drew so much of its strength. This gentleman had been left an orphan at the age of twelve, and he became an apprentice in the P & O Company in the early 1850s. He was appointed to the s.s. *Simla*, the first screw steamship in that company's service, and in her he sailed to the Crimea in 1854, when she transported the heavy cavalry to that campaign.

In 1868 Mr. Creasy left the sea on appointment to the P & O Company's office at Galle. Here his main duty was to accept and send written and semaphore signals from and to ships on the Colombo–Australia run, as Colombo was the nearest cable station to Sydney. In the early 1870s the P & O Company was reconstructed and Mr. Creasy was one of those who had to look for other work. There followed a variety of employment within the island until in 1878, his then employers having succumbed in the coffee crash, Mr. Creasy founded his own business.

Since the Japanese war, Creasy's were for a time the largest exporters of cocoa beans from Ceylon. A Colombo manager of the post-war years has recorded that "Cocoa was first introduced into Ceylon at the beginning of the nineteenth century during the Dutch occupation of the Island. There are, however, no records of any cocoa being exported during the Dutch occupation and it was left to the British to develop both the cultivation and marketing of cocoa. The first recorded export was in 1878 when some 12 cwts was shipped abroad, but in 1955 Ceylon's exports totalled approximately 3000 tons to a value of £900,000. . . . The acreage suitable for cocoa plantations is limited in Ceylon, as cocoa cannot successfully be grown below 500 feet or above 2000 feet elevation and, further, an average annual rainfall of between sixty and eighty inches must be assured if good quality cocoa is to be produced."

From one 'cuppa' to another. In 1953 Steels purchased the firm of Darley Butler & Co. Ltd., blenders and exporters of tea and importers of sundry merchandise—founded in 1847, and probably the oldest business in Colombo. It is suprising, perhaps, that in their hundred Asian years Steels' direct involvement in the tea trade should have come so late in the story.

More recently, nationalistic aspirations have decreed that Darley Butler's become a subsidiary of E. B. Creasy & Company, and that 51 per cent of the equity of the latter be held by Ceylonese nationals. So be it, but there remains to Steels an active, forward-looking interest in the island.

*   *   *

In 1936, success in Ceylon spurred the opening of a rice import branch at Cochin on the Malabar coast of South India. There a new all-year-round port had been constructed which, it was anticipated, would handle most of the imported Burma rice required by the labour on the vast tea and rubber estates up-country. Hitherto this trade had been handled by Indian shippers who bought ex-Steels' mills in Burma, but it now became reasonable to assume that Steels themselves could develop this trade more satisfactorily by selling direct to consumers on the lines successfully established in Ceylon. In this endeavour they received considerable support from old friends and associates in James Finlay & Company, whose subsidiaries operated large acreages under tea in Travancore. Nevertheless, and unlike Ceylon where control was more centralised and the supply area less scattered, it was found difficult to compete with Indian shippers; and as volume business was slow in developing, it was decided after two years' operation to close down the Cochin branch. Be it noted, by critics of Britain's commercial incursions into the Far East, that British companies were always exposed to defeat on the field of trade.

In the context of this story, a mention of the Malabar coast that passed over the name of Peirce Leslie & Co. Ltd. would do no justice. However, among the giants of the coast and 'centurians' in their own right, their 'marriage' with Steels in the final year of this chronicle is described elsewhere.

*   *   *

At the head of the Arabian Sea, the port of Karachi became a fortuitous link between The Attock Oil Company in the Punjab and the outer world, when the bloody events of 1947 raised the religious wall which created Pakistan as a severed limb of what for so long had been a united India. Apart from its services to Attock, the Karachi branch trades today in conditions made no easier by recurrent internecine strife and, like Burma, Pakistan has chosen to withdraw from the Commonwealth of Nations. The most hopeful reflection to be made, perhaps, is that personal relationships have survived the strain.

*   *   *

It has already been made clear that the original *raison d'être* of the pre-war Indian branches at Calcutta, Chittagong and Bombay was the provision of filling installations for and to distribute the petroleum products of the Indo-Burma Petroleum Company's Burma oilfields. It goes without saying that wider activities were always sought.

Calcutta for many years imported from Rangoon small consignments of teak scantlings to the order, among others, of Gladstone Wyllie & Co. Ltd., the employers of William Strang Steel until he left them in favour of distinguished independence. There was occasional business in rice and soap from Steels' Burma sources and, during the twenty-five years of the Assam involvement earlier described, the Calcutta office was caught up to a major extent and mustered quite a large staff. In general terms, however, the hold on the market of local brands was too strong to permit of profitable import dealing. Throughout, the agencies for a number of large insurance companies followed naturally upon similar representation in Burma.

Bombay's operation followed a similar pattern, but was subject to the same restrictions. Until the Second World War the Bombay office was the importing and clearing agency for The Attock Oil Company, a sizeable role which it lost to Karachi when Pakistan attained independence. Subsequent developments and ultimate closure have been mentioned in a previous chapter. But let there also be recall of Bombay's role as a staging post for travellers bound further East: of a hospitable staff ever ready to succour families stranded by transit lacunae: and of the Manager who, unrehearsed and apprehensive—and at the height of communal rioting—took his place in front of the altar to give away a Steels' bride.

Chittagong, perhaps, was the most variously active of the three branches. As agents there for the Scindia Steam Navigation Co. Ltd., Steels had the occasional opportunity to bring in from Burma full cargoes of rice whenever the rice crops in the hinterland fell short of local needs. As pre-war agents for the Hajibhoy Aden Salt Works, Steels' imports, though given to wide fluctuation, could be as high as 25,000 bulk tons a year. Salt is a product subject to excise duty in India once it is committed to a bonded warehouse. As the ships from Aden were invariably chartered for the specific purpose of carrying salt, maximum advantage of laydays was taken by importing agents to sell as much as possible over the side of the ship into rail wagons, lighters and other river craft. Sometimes it was found possible to dispose of over half the cargo excise-free in this manner, and though it was very hectic it was very rewarding.

Post-1947, Chittagong became the port of East Pakistan and, under link with Karachi in the west wing of the country, Steels continued to do a considerable import-export business and to operate a large motor workshop as agents for the Ford Motor Co. of Canada Ltd. However, with the end of Steels' connection with I.B.P., the mainstay of Chittagong's activities was removed, and the branch has been closed down since the end of the century here narrated.

*   *   *

In 1894, Alfred J. P. Baumann bought out the London business of a general merchant dealing mainly in the import of hides and skins, initially from India and

South Africa but increasingly from East Africa as time went on. At the outset he changed the name of his company to A. Baumann & Company.

For many years Baumannn traded almost single-handed from London, but, in an era of rapidly improving communications, he found it necessary to establish a forward base in East Africa. He had been joined in 1923 by his son Eric, and in 1926 he engaged a Mr. Jean Colinvaux, who had resigned from the already well-established East African firm of Leslie & Anderson Ltd., and who sailed for East Africa in that year in order to open Baumann's first overseas branch in Mombasa, the principal sea port of Kenya. This beginning was followed within a few years by the establishment of other branches at Dar-es-Salaam in Tanganyika (now Tanzania) and at Kampala in Uganda. The stage for the future growth of the business was set.

In 1931 Baumann took others into partnership, Eric and Colinvaux among them, and in 1948 they transferred the whole of the assets to a limited liability company incorporated in Kenya, with the London partnership as a wholly-owned subsidiary. Simultaneously Steels acquired a substantial minority interest in the Kenya company and thenceforward shared in the day-to-day management of the company. In 1952 Alfred Baumann died, having visited East Africa but once during the fifty-eight years of his connection. Shortly thereafter the head office was transferred from Mombasa to Nairobi and Baumanns became—and still is— a public, quoted company in Kenya.

In the 1950's much of Baumanns' profits came from the company's coffee-processing factories and cotton-trading interests in Uganda and from coffee and produce trading in Kenya and Tanganyika; but these activities ceased progressively when between 1961 and 1963 the three countries attained independence and declared themselves Republics within the British Commonwealth. Thenceforward local interests received preferential treatment in coffee processing and Baumanns were excluded from further participation in what had been a major part of their Uganda business. In 1970 Steels acquired an additional shareholding such as made Baumanns a subsidiary company.

At this significant point in time, the final years of Steels' century, a reference to Appendix B will show the extent to which the Baumann 'empire' had expanded and diversified. The activities of Baumanns' subsidiary companies included the import and sale of industrial equipment and foodstuffs and the distribution of locally-produced cement and foodstuffs. Refrigerated stores were operated in Nairobi, Mombasa and Nakuru, while a provender mill in Nakuru still produces cattle, pig, poultry and dog foods. Through Leslie & Anderson (East Africa) Ltd., acquired by Baumanns in 1967, are conducted shipping and general agencies; and through their subsidiary, Wafco Ltd., a warehousing and forwarding business.

Perhaps Baumanns' most colourful activity is the magnificent farm, 'Milmet' of 1780 acres, which, on three occasions out of five, has won the Kenya Agricultural Society's tri-ennially awarded gold medal for the best mixed farm in Kenya. Here are grown coffee, barley and citrus fruits, while a large area of grazing land carries herds of dairy and beef cattle.

Through associated partnership companies, Baumanns have interest in paint factories with the Leyland Paint Company of Leyland, Lancashire, in refriger-

Coffee picking, Kenya

Some of the herd at "Milmet"

Silage harvesting at "Milmet"

ation, engineering and contracting with Hall Thermotank, and in tea blending and export with Mathesons. Gone are the skins and hides of yesteryear.

Steels' forest venture on the Rondo plateau of Tanganyika has been described in the Timber Department chapter. Another enterprise, conducted in partnership with the Uganda Government and with Baumanns, was the clearing of a large area of jungle in Bunyoro for the planting of cotton, groundnuts and other products on a tenant-farming basis. Unfortunately, like the British Government's earlier and large-scale East African groundnuts scheme of sorry memory, clearing costs were too heavy to support and the scheme, as it was intended, died after a few years of hard work. It is pleasing to relate, however, that most of the area cleared still serves the Uganda Government as a cottonseed multiplication farm.

East African operations today are carried on within the three independent nations already named, but not without complications born of the sharply contrasting political and ideological stars that each seeks to follow. However, it is not for the first time that Steels find themselves operating against such a background, and Baumann's East African group is endowed with a built-in flexibility designed to absorb as best possible 'the slings and arrows of outrageous fortune'.

CHAPTER VII

THE MIDDLE EAST AND THE MEDITERRANEAN

Steels' interest in the Middle East was roused, not surprisingly, by the prospects for trade in rice. From very early days the Levant had been an important market for Burma rice, and in 1934 representatives of Steels and the other 'London Shippers' made a visit of reconnaissance to Palestine, the outcome of which was the floating of the Palestine Milling and Trading Company Limited. In 1936 the combine built a rice mill in Haifa, to which a member of Steels' staff was posted as manager.

In 1939 Steels acquired an interest in Sulphur Quarries Limited, which held concessions over a large area of sulphur deposits near Gaza. In 1944 the company was disposed of owing to technical difficulties in refining the sulphur to an acceptable degree of purity; but the seemingly negative venture bred a longer-term gain, in view of world events to follow, in that it led to Steels establishing their own office in Haifa.

In the middle of 1940, when Europe was largely under the domination of the Nazi jackboot, Steels were asked by the Mandated Government of Palestine, with the approval of the Colonial Office, to act as Government agents for the receiving, storage and distribution of foodstuffs. This was a task of such magnitude as to demand an expansion of Steels' staff in the country from three to nearly a thousand; but, in the next five years, they handled some 1,200,000 tons of food of a sales value of some £50,000,000—this at a time when Rommel strode the North African desert, the U-boats were sinking enormous tonnages of merchant shipping along the approaches to the Mediterranean, and the Italians' *mare nostrum* itself, within bomber reach of all its shores, was a Tom Tiddler's ground for any who ventured upon its waters. By the end of the Mandate in 1948, the tonnage of food handled had exceeded two million tons.

Apart from the importing aspect of Steels' task, there were vast problems of collection and distribution within Palestine itself. The country was precariously deficient in crop foodstuffs. Trans-Jordan, on the other hand, was a surplus producer. Towards the end of 1942 the Palestine Government became the sole buyer of Jordan's exportable surplus; and to Steels was left the intricate game of put and take implicit in the buying, collecting and distributing of this surplus. Let imagination try to visualise the task in a countryside poorly served by railways at the best of times and now yielding priority of carriage to the movement of troops and military supplies. To cope with this competition, Government acquired 600 lorries while a further 1700 were conscripted from independent operators. All were placed under Steels' operational control and, apart from their prime role as food carriers, many of them had to be deployed otherwise, assisting in such tasks as the construction of airfields and in the transport of potash from the Dead Sea. In the latter role, the outward trip of the lorries would have been unladen but for arrangements made to send stone from Jerusalem to Shuna, near the northern end of the Dead Sea. There the Emir of Trans-Jordan, later to become King Abdullah of Jordan when his country became independent on termination of the Palestine Mandate, was building his palace. This transport-free assistance was no small service under wartime conditions.

By 1945, through their transport agency, Steels were carrying a larger tonnage than the railways. All this activity involved them in opening additional offices at Jaffa, Tel Aviv, Jerusalem, Nazareth, Gaza, Beirut and Damascus—with extensive garages and workshops at the larger of these bases.

These mechanical facilities, however, were not all-embracing in their function. They had little relevance, for example, to the procurement from Iraq of meat on the hoof—mainly camels and sheep. They could do nothing in the matter of educating local populaces in the eating of the orange. Oranges have never been an item of diet in Trans-Jordan and many areas of Palestine; but with wartime conditions totally frustrating the traditional export of the citrus crop—the famous Jaffa orange—the eating of it locally had to be encouraged, like it or not. Domestic consumption, however, fell far short of the exportable surplus and it became necessary to pay the owners of groves in Jaffa, Jerusalem and elsewhere three pounds a ton of oranges merely to pick the fruit off the trees and drop it on to the ground.

Then again, garages have no part to play in the life of the fish: but here let speak Geoffrey Morgan Shipton (1947–1963). Shipton's Middle East experience pre-dated by many years his joining the staff of Steels, and it had included several years of service with Spinneys Limited, an internationally known provisioning company trading in the Levant, the story of whose subsequent association with Steels is told later in this chapter. What follows is an extract from Shipton's account of a strangely hybrid venture—

In 1942 Spinneys were asked by the British Mandated Government of Palestine to act as Government Agents for their new project, the 'Akaba Fisheries'. In short, this project was to catch, freeze, transport and sell to the public of Palestine fish from the Gulf of Akaba. Spinneys were concerned in the catching, freezing and sale, but Steel Brothers, as the Government Transport Agents, in the transport.

At the time every avenue to increase the food supplies without calling on our over-taxed shipping had to be explored, so with the assistance of the British Army, in the persons of the Royal Engineers, the following scheme was evolved.

The R.E.s would build a cold store at Akaba, and Spinneys were to install the machinery; the Palestine Government were to provide a ship, in which again Spinneys were to install freezing chambers. The fish was to be caught in the Gulf, frozen on the ship, taken to Akaba, and kept in the cold store pending transport by Steel Brothers,

95

in insulated boxes, across the Sinai Desert to Palestine for sale throughout the country.

The theoretics were grand, but let us see what happened in practice. It must, of course, be realised that this project was started at the lowest ebb of our national fight for world freedom, and construction supplies of all kinds were extremely hard to come by. Cork for insulation, to quote just one example, had largely to be replaced by a form of blown concrete which might work on dry land, but on a ship left much to be desired.

The first trouble was that the foundations for the cold store, which were built on the edge of the Gulf, disappeared into the Gulf after one very stormy night and the work had to be started all over again. Then the ship, the *Doron*, a kyak built locally, turned out to be the most unhandy vessel that could have been discovered. Firstly its engine was underpowered and against a four-knot wind the ship would invariably go backwards; and then, with all sails set, it tended to capsize in anything over a light breeze. The other headache was that, not being copper sheathed, after three months in the Gulf the weight of barnacles and other sea accretions that attached themselves nearly foundered the craft.

The question of fishing was always the most difficult. It was decided to establish little fishing stations and induce local fishermen to catch fish and *langouste* which they would put into insulated boxes provided with ice, and every four days the *Doron* would call round and collect the fish. With the strong winds and currents, usual breakdowns, etc., the *Doron* was often a few days late, by which time, in that heat, the fish had gone off a little more than somewhat! . . .

There was, of course, the ever-present headache of trans-desert transport. We fitted up two lorries with huge insulated boxes, the weight of which cut down the pay-load by half, and many a time the lorries were unable to make the tough grade up out of Akaba on to the desert plateau. This meant a shuttle service with fish to the top, which on a blazing hot day soon softened up a couple of tons of fish.

The question of fishing rights also had to be solved, for the best fish came from the Saudi Arabian side. In the early stages, whenever the *Doron* approached within half a mile of their coast, it became the regular practice for the local tribesmen to send a few bullets whistling over and around the ship. . . .

There is an interjection called for here in this recital of wartime activities in Palestine. As a background to Steels' and Spinney's dynamic execution of their fortuitous and varied tactical roles, there is discernible evidence of much official strategic genius. Historically the servants of the Mandated Government of Palestine were not the first strangers in this troubled area of the globe to be called upon to make bricks without straw; and not always does one speak kindly of bureaucracy: but here is an outstanding example of competent and devoted execution of authority in extremely daunting conditions. Fortunately we are able to include as an appendix to this story a reciprocal compliment written at the end of the war by Geoffrey Walsh, the Palestine Government Food Controller of the day, who later, as Financial Secretary, was to die when the King David Hotel in Jerusalem was blown up.

With the end of the world war came for Palestine the tortured chapter of terror and strife that marked the precipitate termination in 1948 of twenty-five years of British mandated government. While Steels' staff elsewhere were coming to terms with peacetime living, those in Palestine had had to evacuate their wives and children to Cyprus and Lebanon and themselves were risking the sniper's bullet between office and abode, or the saboteur's mine under bridge or building when on tour.

As 1947 ran into 1948, the intensity of the fighting between Arabs and Jews in Haifa increased. Early in April 1948, to meet the possible emergency of an evacuation, Steels chartered a landing craft which was available in the port. It was none too soon because, in the middle of the month, without advance warning, the British forces withdrew from the town to positions in the port and on Mount Carmel. This withdrawal was the opportunity for battle to commence in the *souks* between highly trained Jewish forces and ill-equipped Arabs. There could never have been any doubt about the outcome, and by late April long convoys of Arab refugees were in flight northward to Lebanon, the nearest haven of safety. Steels' contingency plan had then to be put into effect.

Elsewhere in this story, J. B. Clark has described the task that fell to him during the evacuation of Burma in 1942. That he was on hand with a companion account of events in Palestine six years later establishes him as an unwitting authority on popular disaster. Taken from his writings is this distressing fragment—

> Standing at the entrance to the port to identify our Arab staff and their families, I felt very sad to see them leaving their homes probably for ever, and many of them were in tears as they looked at their beloved Haifa for the last time. Fortunately for them we were able to fix up jobs elsewhere and they now seem quite prosperous again. For nearly one million of their Arab brothers the position is very dismal and one wonders what the solution to this refugee problem is finally going to be.

A quarter of a century later the question remains unanswered.

The few British staff who remained in Haifa were able to perform humanitarian service to the refugees by arranging for the re-shipment from Haifa to Beirut and onward to Amman of goods to the value of over a million pounds which had become blocked in Haifa by the closure of the railway to Amman. Such an operation could never have been wholly successful because many imports of strategic value had already been commandeered by the Jewish forces by the time the shipping documents had been entrusted to Steels. In such cases, however, Steels' certification that they had been instructed to arrange shipment, but that the goods could not be traced in Haifa, was accepted by underwriters in London and New York, in every case it is believed, as earnest that the consignees had done all in their power to recover their goods.

Steels' landing craft completed the evacuation to Beirut of the company's Arab staff and families and the bare necessities they carried with them. It then returned to Haifa and did several more round trips to Beirut carrying Jordan cargo before the Haifa port came under Jewish control at the end of June.

Thus, with a world war behind them, did Steels' staff in Palestine survive during this grotesque period. The hazards of life, even for the neutral, need no stressing, for the bullet and the bomb are no respecter of persons; but there was a remarkable degree of acceptance of their presence. What better example could there be than the experience of a member of the staff who, about to board a bus, had a friendly Arab sidle up and whisper—"Don't take that one, Sir. We're blowing it up down the road"?

Clark was awarded the M.B.E. for his services in Palestine. If the end, for Steels, was one more withdrawal, it was hardly without honour.

✲   ✲   ✲

Arthur Rawdon Spinney was a cavalry officer in Allenby's Palestine Army during the war of 1914–1918. After the armistice and the avalanche of demobili-

97

sation that followed it, he found himself, like many thousands of others, faced with a prospect that no longer carried with it an assurance of keep and clothing, whatever the attendant hazards; a prospect that compelled, without loss of time, that one's own talent for initiative be explored and exploited; for no longer was life to be a years' old matter of acting on orders.

Spinney stayed with what he had learnt—the Middle East. Perhaps, in essence, it was a soldier's choice, for the area in which he chose to operate has never ceased to be a battle ground in one sense or another. His strategic concept was the supply of domestic needs in an area of impoverishment, poor communications and climatic discomfort: his tactical approach was the establishment of trading posts wherever this object could best be served.

Spinney's reputation was first established in the Levant, Jordan and Iraq where, subject to the interruption imposed by the renewed march of armies in 1939–1945, his trading has been carried on for half a century. Cyprus was added to the list in the thirties.

With the rapid revelation of the Middle East as the biggest reservoir of crude petroleum in the world, Spinney's sphere widened immeasurably and it was not long before he held a dominant position in the supply of what used to be known as 'oilman's stores' to the many fields that were drilled in the area and to the refineries that followed them.

The Second World War reduced Spinney's operation to a catch-as-catch-can activity, dominated variously by army control and enemy occupation and, obviously, by the all-round reduction in vital supplies imposed by the conditions of total war. Nevertheless, considerable ingenuity was displayed in seeking out new sources of supply and in popularising hitherto unregarded or unacceptable forms of food. Shortages notwithstanding—and it was a situation to gladden the heart of a profiteer—Spinney stuck to a policy of controlled costing which earned for his company a reputation of never taking advantage of public needs. This policy has been scrupulously followed ever since, and the benefits in popular appreciation have been immense.

After the war, the prospects for Spinneys on a wider stage were plain for all to see, and in 1948 the business was reorganised, emerging as Spinney's (1948) Ltd., with headquarters initially at Beirut in the Lebanon and later at Baghdad in Iraq. Nationalistic aspirations, and the increasingly severe currency barriers resulting therefrom, dictated that expansion must take the form of self-financing, locally staffed and registered subsidiary or associated companies as particular circumstances demanded.

First came a business started in Kuwait in partnership with Yusuf Al Ghanim, a prominent local business man. This union blossomed into a very active agency and commission business—the Gulf Trading & Refrigerating Company. In 1951 Spinneys stepped up their operations in Iraq by acquiring a majority interest in W. J. Coker & Company. Coker, like Spinney, had had a military introduction to the Middle East and, on demobilisation, he started in business there, first on the staff of a company successfully handling the Ford agency and then, in 1926, on his own account in the same line of business. By the time he sold out to Spinneys, a planned move to facilitate his retirement, his company was one of the largest and best known in Iraq. In 1952, likewise in Iraq, Spinneys floated a

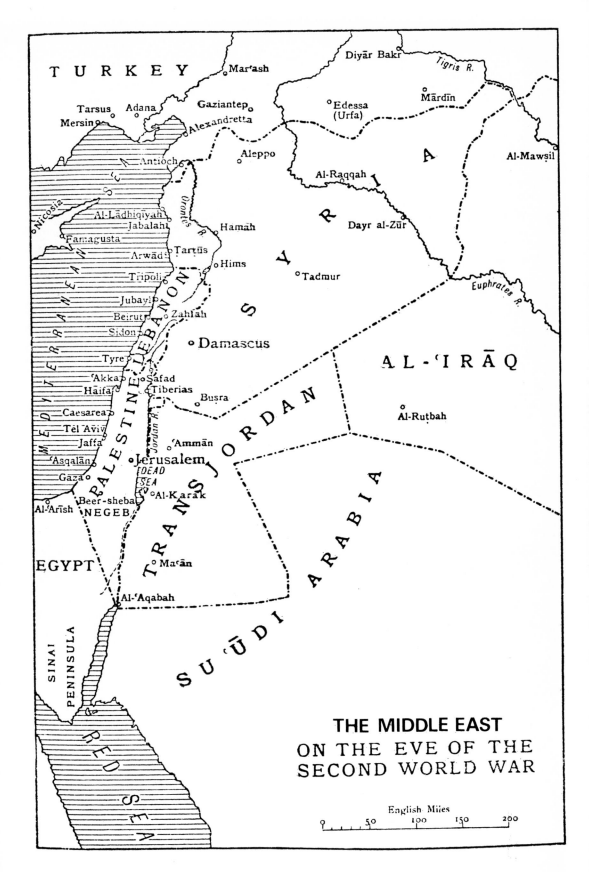

The Middle East on the eve of the Second World War

Steels' staff in Palestine during the Mandate
J. B. Clark, J. H. Gaunt, B. J. Green, J. M. Smith, J. C. Highet, W. F. G.
Salkeld, J. S. Pringle, W. B. Somerville, J. S. Cook;
Mesdames Highet, Green, Cook; T. O. M. Pope (manager), Mesdames Pope,
Gaunt, Pringle

Some of the six hundred—Palestine, 1943

Small beginnings:

Spinneys at Dubai, 1961   Spinneys Store at Abu Dhabi, 1962

Spinneys Centre, Beirut

subsidiary company, Rafidain Developments Ltd., to develop business in tractors and other agricultural plant. After a chequered start the company was taken over by Steels and traded prosperously for a number of years until 1967 when, under a newly promulgated law, it had to be sold to Iraqi interests. Also in 1952 came Spinneys' establishment of their Aden branch to operate a big provisioning contract called for by the construction of the Aden oil refinery (and how well remembered, by birds of passage whose roots lay further east, are Spinneys' Aden staff for occasions of personal assistance).

References to Spinneys and 'provisioning' have been made so far without definition. In the context of the Aden refinery we have it that—"Aden, being in an unwatered desert area, fresh fruit, vegetables and dairy produce have been hard to come by. To augment the slender local supples, therefore, these require-ments have been flown in from Eritrea in considerable quantities on regular twice-a-week flights. Ready-cut frozen meat is imported in large quantities from Australia: sheep are brought in from British Somaliland on the hoof and are slaughtered as required at the slaughter-house. From Kenya come eggs and bacon, from Italy fine cheeses, fresh fruits and tomato products, from South Africa canned fruit juices, etc. In all, supplies have been drawn from some twenty-two different countries, and at the peak of construction food was arriving in Aden port at the rate of a consignment a day. By the end of construction, approximately 14,000 tons of foodstuffs will have been handled."

Clearly it was not at Spinneys that G. K. Chesterton aimed when he wrote—

> He sells us sands of Araby
> As sugar for cash down;
> He sweeps his shop and sells the dust
> The purest salt in town,
> He crams with cans of poisoned meat
> Poor subjects of the King,
> And when they die by thousands
> Why, he laughs like anything.

In rapid succession to Aden followed a partnership with Ali Bin Ali in Qatar and the opening of further trading stations at Dubai, Abu Dhabi, Sharjah and Oman, in which last-named State business was based on a partnership with the long-established firm of W. J. Towell & Company. In the Gulf area, also, Spinneys purchased the business of J. H. Rayner & Company of Bahrein, thereby rounding off a trading involvement with most of the Arab side of the Gulf.

Let there be no assumption of saturation. In 1960 Spinneys penetrated Libya and Algeria, working commissary contracts for newly developing oilfields and pipeline construction projects. A few years later there was involvement in the provisioning of North Sea drilling rigs, in no way more convincingly, though tragically, illustrated by the fact that when the marine rig *Sea Gem* collapsed and disappeared in violent weather in 1965, four of the thirteen who died with her were men of Spinneys. In 1966 came a partnership with Michel Doumet, a prominent Lebanese business man, in the erection and operation in Beirut of a supermarket which is the equal of any to be found anywhere.

The union of Steels and Spinneys was not an affair of absorption by trading conquest, but a matter of mutual accommodation and consolidation. It was initiated in 1948 when Steels bought a half interest in Spinneys and injected their Middle East interests into the Spinneys organisation. Increasingly, trading conditions in the Mediterranean basin promoted a mutuality of purpose, and it was no more than logical that in 1967 Steels should purchase the balance of Spinneys' equity. Spinneys' Managing Director, James Taylor Wishart, joined Steels' Board and a year later was appointed an executive Director—the first man in the company's history to have had no service as a member of Steels' staff junior to that level. Equally it was no more than common sense that Spinneys have continued to trade under the name that has become a household word in their specialized role in their particular sphere. Be it acknowledged—there was little that Steels could teach them!

Since 1967, Spinneys' reputation as purveyors of 'oilman's stores' has extended to off-shore drilling operations in the Far East, around the Mediterranean and in Africa; and at least a preliminary probe has been made for the prospects developing in this line in Western Australia. More of them will be heard in the story of Steels' second century.

CHAPTER VIII
CANADA

In Steels' House Magazine of December 1951 it was recorded that "Mr. McCreath, accompanied by Mrs. McCreath, has just returned from an enjoyable if strenuous two months tour of Canada where, with the able assistance of E. S. Millar and E. S. Pinfold, he has been examining the possibilities of our establishing ourselves in that prosperous and hospitable Dominion."

McCreath and Pinfold have already found place in the Oil Department's story; and since Ebenezer Simpson Millar (1913–1950) had been General Manager of The Attock Oil Company from 1931 to 1942, the target which prompted the reconnaissance is self-evident. However, it was not on the derrick floor that the arrow was to find its mark.

Before developing the Canadian theme, however, there is a point to be made if posterity is to be served and the story is not to be read as the biography of a steamroller. 2070's chronicler, when writing of Canada, seems likely to find himself treating largely of Steel Brothers Canadian Holdings Ltd. Historically it would be wrong, at this opportunity, to introduce otherwise than as distinct entities the companies which have come within the carapace during nearly twenty years of association thus far. Particularly is this so while their pioneering roots are still a matter of clear record and justifiable family pride.

In 1953 it was recorded that Gavin Muir (1947–1956) "having returned from leave, has disappeared to Calgary, Canada." Thus briefly had Steels established a first footing in a land wherein their experience of hostile expulsion elsewhere was a trading hazard now to merit scant consideration. The event was soon followed by the opening of a Branch office in Vancouver and the establishment there of a new appointment—General Manager, Canada.

*   *   *

As with other ventures described in this story, the origins of Loders Lime Company Limited lie somewhere between the colourful and the legendary. But so often does the apocryphal illumine the authentic that we would be missing something if we did not borrow Muir's historical note—

The history of the early days of the lime operations at Kananaskis, fifty-eight miles west of Calgary, appears full of uncertainty. Strange tales are told of the original owner having mysteriously disappeared on the trail to Calgary and the founder of the company, Walter Loder, who was a worker on the property, inheriting it. In those days lime was burned in brick kilns which were situated along the main Canadian Pacific Railway line to the west, and the output was mainly sold to the railway.

All this, however, is quite unsubstantiated and as far as official records show, the firm of Loders was first incorporated in 1906 with the assistance mainly of British capital and the plant constructed at our present site.

In the early days this company's lime was burnt by means of wood, which is reputed to give the best plaster lime possible, and a flourishing business was created amongst the local Stoney Indians who supplied cords of wood to keep the three kilns operating.

The business remained on a small scale because of lack of industrial development in the Western Provinces up to Mr. Loder's death in 1936. In 1938 the control of Loders was acquired by a Mr. Garnett. Mr. Garnett was an active man in the sales field in Alberta, and with the rapid expansion of the Province's industries, he developed operations at Loders until his death in 1948. After this date, until late in 1952, the business was managed by Mrs. Garnett and had the distinction of being one of the few companies in Canada operated by a woman. In October 1952, Messrs Steel Brothers & Company Limited and the National Mining Corporation Limited purchased from Mrs. Garnett the control of this company and so gave the business a new lease of life.

Happily Muir's note stands to be supplemented by the independent research of a rising Canadian star among contributors to Steels House Magazine. Mabel Jordon, wife of the then Plant Superintendent at Kananaskis, provided in 1957 an article from which the following is borrowed—

From the meagre records available it is apparent that lime kilns were in operation at Kananaskis before the transcontinental railway reached there in 1884. And, contrary to local legend, the business was not started by the Loder brothers. A Scottish settler named McCanleish first saw the potential opportunity there for the lime. He knew, of course, that the railway would soon be completed, with the inevitable result of population increase. . . .

By 1888 the business was well established. The town of Calgary and other settlements in southern Alberta provided a ready market. One day during that year a young Englishman who had been working as a woodcutter on the railway near Banff was wending his way eastward toward Calgary seeking new employment. In passing Kananaskis he stopped to ask if work was available. McCanleish quickly hired him as an expert woodcutter for the ever-hungry kiln fires. This itinerant Englishman had been in the British Merchant Navy before migrating to Canada. His name was Ed. Loder.

He stayed on at Kananaskis and learned the various phases of the lime business. Just how he actually acquired control is not clear, but the story is that McCanleish went off to Calgary one day leaving Loder in charge, and never returned. Be that as it may, Loder did acquire the business with a brother as a partner. The two Eds., Edwin and Edward Loder, got squatters' rights to the property and built several more kilns east of the present Kananaskis station. They operated under the name of Loder Brothers until 1905.

Since 1952, the oil boom, the pulp industry, the mineral discoveries in British Columbia and the Northern Territories, and the growth of petro-chemical and other industries in Alberta have combined to promote an upsurge in industrial activity in the Western Provinces. The resultant substantial increase in the demand for lime has been measured and met by Loders in developments modern, costly and successful.

First to be revolutionised, in 1957, were the lime quarrying methods of early days, now becoming archaic. The advance of any cut into a hillside by conventional 'terracing' methods becomes complicated in increasing proportion to the demands both of safety and of efficient extraction. As the height of the working face rises and the succession of terraces increases, the width of the adit—the only thing left to 'give'—narrows. That way, eventually, lies underground mining.

There was much, at the time, that was still experimental in the technique of 'longhole' drilling as adopted. This method discards the piece-meal approach that is terracing, relying instead on a top-to-bottom drilling of shot holes, suitably angled from the vertical to yield a safely sloped face rather than a cliff. Such drilling, down to 150 feet per hole at Kananaskis, is costly of course, but the harvest is substantial. 18,000 tons of broken limestone on the quarry floor was the yield from one of the early tests. Needless to say the technique was adopted and still prevails.

There followed, in 1967, the production at Kananaskis (Exshaw) of lime from almost the first rotary lime kiln in Western Canada, with all the benefits of flexibility and quality control that stem from such a costly installation. The kiln measures 165 feet in length by 10 feet in diameter. Output is some 240 tons daily, bagged or in bulk according to purpose. It meets the needs of steel mills, the construction industry, water treatment plants, paper manufacture and a host of lesser claimants, not only in Alberta but in neighbouring Provinces.

There are no predictable limits to continuing expansion. McCanleish? The Loders? They are gone from the scene but, like others in this story, they founded far beyond their dreams.

*   *   *

Diversification does not always spell success, and the story of Ytong is that of a promising tree that died, perhaps because its roots were not Canadian.

Alberta Ytong Manufacturing Company Limited was sponsored by Canadian and British interests under Steels' management. The project was aimed at introducing to Canada, by on-the-spot manufacture, a light-weight, cellular concrete building block developed in Sweden and proven for over a quarter of a century in that country and, post-war, in Britain, Germany and other European countries. The Canadian factory was built at Calgary in 1954 under Swedish supervision, and technicians were brought across from Sweden to bring the plant into operation.

Government projects, high-rise apartments and commercial buildings should have provided a ready market for the finished product because of its lightness and its heating-cum-soundproofing advantages; but it was the wider field of home building that had to be won before the project could become viable. Here it was that the challenge of Ytong was met and mastered by the availability of a plentiful supply of cheap natural gas for heating purposes. This made it possible for the traditional timber frame house to maintain its popularity over the more expensive Ytong product, the other advantages of which domestically were not so relevant. It was also the existence of an extensive and viable concrete block industry which prevented the company getting a firm foothold in the building market. In 1967 the Ytong plant was closed down, victim to a gift of Nature that played no part in success or failure in Europe.

*   *   *

Another failure was the Hope Lumber Company, but this, unfortunately, was largely a case of Steels being outmanoeuvred. The first step was the purchase of a sawmill at Hope, about a hundred miles east of Vancouver, on the basis that accessible forest concessions were due to be auctioned by Government. When the auction took place, Steels were bid up by a Canadian-domiciled Sikh who went to a price well beyond the limit that Steels' Manager had been authorised to pay.

There remained the alternative of bidding for more distant concessions, but the cost of extracting and moving lumber to the mill would have been excessive. Finally Steels had to face negotiating with the successful bidder, who asked and received a price that gave him a handsome profit. At the time, the mid-fifties, lumber prices were at a peak which was to be maintained for years afterwards. On top of this, and the premium purchase price, Government rates of royalty were high. A losing struggle continued until 1962, when the mill was closed and the company wound up.

*   *   *

Rex and Roy Dales, identical twins, earned a living driving trucks for others until the Second World War, when both served overseas with the Royal Canadian Air Force. On demobilisation they pooled their resources and bought three trucks wherewith to start their own haulage business—gravel in summer, lumber in winter.

Further investment in a second-hand tractor loader nearly proved disastrous. They hired it to Government to load gravel, but so frequently did it break down that they were asked to remove it. Repairing and operating it themselves, they obtained in 1949 the lease of a gravel pit near Edmonton, and here they put the tractor to work extracting and loading gravel. Thus, fortuitously and precariously, did the brothers enter the sand and gravel business on their own account.

They prospered by dint of hard work, and within six years their annual turnover was running at over $600,000. The fleet of three trucks had given place to one of eleven. The original, temperamental tractor loader had been succeeded by a new one. Two draglines and a crusher had been bought, the latter enabling the brothers to expand into the crushed road gravel business. Leases were acquired over more gravel pits. In 1953 the company of Dales Bros. Ltd. was incorporated. Prospects in the concrete gravel field beckoned as industry and building in Alberta spawned. Such breakneck expansion, inevitably, was arrested by the need for capital, and in 1955 Steels acquired a share in the business which later was to become wholly theirs. But thus are foundations laid.

The immediate programme called for the erection of a large gravel plant at Onoway, some thirty miles west of Edmonton, where large deposits of gravel were known to exist. Construction of the plant was started in November 1955, and six months later it was 'on stream'. It was of modern design, capable of crushing, washing and screening four different sizings of rocks at a rate of nearly 300 tons per hour. Water for the operation is pumped from a nearby creek with the fortuitous assistance of beavers, whose appropriately sited dam helps to maintain the water level. May it not be in Canada, as seems ordained for so much animal life elsewhere, that posterity should ask 'what was a beaver?'.

In 1956, on eleven acres of land purchased in Edmonton, an office and workshop were erected and provision was made for the stock-piling of gravel from the

The Exshaw Lime Plant, Onoway, Canada

Onoway plant. A fleet of fifteen trucks and trailers was acquired to carry the plant's output to Edmonton, and the first season's operation raised the company's turnover to above a million dollars. In retrospect that was no more than a beginning.

In current terms, Dales Brothers is the backbone of the Aggregates Division of Steel Brothers Canada Ltd. From Lorne R. Reesor, writing in 1969 as Manager of the Division, we have it that—

> Aggregates Division is the largest independent gravel supplier in the Edmonton area and approximately half of our sales are generated from the products consumed by the ready-mix concrete market, our biggest customer being associate company, Forden Concrete Ltd., which uplifts almost all our washed gravel, the remainder, from the 'dry' side (not washed), being used for asphalting and road base materials.
>
> We operate a full complement of gravel crushing equipment, trucks, washing and screening plants for special products.
>
> The washing plant for concrete aggregates is located in Onoway, some 30 miles west of Edmonton, producing half a million tons of material in the seven frost-free months of each year, and that is sufficient to serve the market for the full year. . . .
>
> The 'dry' end of our production is carried out in owned and leased properties in an area north east of Edmonton and some fifteen miles distant from the city centre, all production being through a portable plant capable of out-turning 250 tons per hour. In an average year it will crush 250,000 to 300,000 tons, most of this material being stock-piled and reloaded when sold by rubber-tyred loaders.
>
> Our 'specialty' operations are carried out in the main city yard and there we make available, from our standard washed aggregates, material for concrete mixing, sand for blasting, rock for bonded roofs, rock and sand for water filtration plants, hot dry sand for ice control on airport runways, rock for garden decoration, coloured crushed rock for building panels and stucco. These are only some of the uses served by our products, all of which are processed to satisfy an exacting market, and constant testing is carried out, both departmentally and by independent laboratories, in order to ensure the high quality standards for which the company is recognised.

*　　*　　*

The principal export of Scotland, by long tradition, has been Scots men and women. The Pitkethly family, four sons and four daughters of a far-flung Clan, emigrated to British Columbia just before the First World War and, soon after their arrival, the brothers David and Tom, their combined resources sunk in a horse team, were plying the unpaved streets and wooden sidewalks of Vancouver with wood and coal.

In Scotland, the family on both sides had been associated with the building trade for many generations, and that way—beyond the wood and the coal—lay their real urge. In 1925 the brothers bought eight acres of land on the bank of the North Arm of the Fraser River. By the end of that year their stock-in-trade included five 4-ton trucks and they were excavating for building foundations, still with wood and coal as a longstop. Their excavating contracts persuaded them, as what better could, of the rapidity with which Vancouver was growing, and soon they were in the business of providing building materials.

The eight-acre location they had chosen was ideal for the supply of sand and gravel, and, quite fantastically, they were to have no problem of wasting assets. The Fraser River, from its Rocky Mountains source, brings down millions of tons of sand and gravel, and the accumulations near its mouth are cleared by dredges every three years. As the dredges pass the Pitkethly site they disgorge their massive loads of spoil into a six-acre pit of 660 feet river frontage. Here the sand is separated in screening plants and removed by an ant-like stream of trucks. After three years there is ample accommodation for a refill. Rarely ever can supply and demand have been so felicitously mated.

Inevitably the challenge of expansion led the Pitkethlys into other aspects of the building trade. Notable among these were the manufacture of plastering materials and concrete bricks, but the massive warehouses held over sixty types of building material.

Steels came into the Pitkethly story in 1955 by acquiring a majority interest in the company on the retirement of the elder brother, Tom. Later they took over the remaining family shares when Dave, the driving force, decided to retire. History must record, however, that it was not long before Dave surrendered his retirement in favour of getting back into business on his own account at over seventy years of age.

*   *   *

Loders, Dales, Pitkethlys and now Jordans. The brotherly theme seems to be inseparable from this Canadian chapter—indeed from the story as a whole, for is not the master theme that of the two brothers who put up their trading board in London in 1873?

It is recorded in Steels' *House Magazine* that—

> This company was founded in 1945 by Joe Jordan of Vancouver, whose brother Norman joined him in the same year, and named Jordan's Machineworks Ltd., the entire initial capital of $100,000 being put up by the Jordan Brothers and their mother, so it was very much a private concern. Originally the plan was to construct, starting from the raw material, heavy-duty machines suitable for use mainly in the arduous conditions found in the Canadian logging and lumber industries. Such machines were, and still are, manufactured and marketed by the company under the 'Blu-Chip'—a very appropriate—brand name.
>
> In the early days not only fork-lifts but a regular assortment of machines was manu-factured—compressors, winches, self-propelling cranes, four-wheel drive trucks—in fact anybody having the need for a particular machine could, in all probability, have it tailor-made by Jordan's to his requirement—which says much for the skills of the Jordan brothers and the team of designers and craftsmen who worked for and with them.
>
> However, and this is a further example of ingenuity on the drawing board, in 1955 'Blu-Chip' introduced one of the first really successful centre-articulated vehicles in North America and, later, this design which makes for quite an astonishing degree of manoeuvrability, was incorporated in the company's full range of fork-lift trucks and mobile cranes.

In 1967 Steels purchased a half interest in Jordan's Machineworks Ltd. under conditions that enabled them to bring to bear their wide experience of manage-ment; and in 1969 they acquired the balance of the capital. Simultaneously the name of the company was changed to Canadian Lift and Loader Ltd. to provide a clearer portrayal of the company's widened and widening role.

1970's production covers a range of first-grade machines of lift capacity from 6000 to 25,000 lbs., two or four-wheel-drive, all using articulated centre steering, and some with rear steering as well to give an even greater degree of manoeuvra-bility. Are we, perchance and belatedly, contemplating here a threat to the dominance of the elephant in the teak forests of Asia?

*   *   *

Steels' Canadian head office at Vancouver controls the activities described as now comprising their Canadian Holdings. Additionally it maintains links as an importer of commodities that are loaded on ship-board by others of the company's interests in East Africa, Ceylon and elsewhere. For a diminishing band can there occasionally be an aroma of nostalgia for bygone days as the hatches are uncovered in the port of Vancouver? After all, and in no conventional or frivolous sense, we are treating of an Eastern company that went West.

By definition, this story of Steels does not extend beyond 1970. Of no other chapter can it be said with such certainty that it will be out-dated by the time it reaches the reader. That is both a tribute to Canada and a recognition by the compiler of this volume that the author of the next will expect him to 'keep off the grass'.

CHAPTER IX

AUSTRALIA

Steels were scouting for prospects in Australia for some years before they made their landfall in 1968—just within the compass of this story of a hundred years. The restraining factor was that the funds earmarked for this expansion were—and still are—frozen by the Government of Burma.

As with Canada, so with Australia; it was the pioneering West that beckoned; a West sundered from an earlier-developed East by prairie in the one case and by desert in the other; both Wests retaining, perhaps, a subtler tie than their Easts with the rocks whence their peoples were hewn. In Canada it was oil and gas that prompted the modern acceleration: in Australia it has been iron ore and nickel. The parallel goes further for, in Australia as in Canada, it was capital-hungry small businesses set for expansion that welcomed Steels' participation; and, again, it was the haulage and construction prospects sparked by the mining boom of the late sixties and early seventies that provided the launching pad.

Steel Brothers (Australia) Limited came to birth in the West by buying and combining, within a period of two years, the businesses of Cornelius Naylor Transport Ltd. (general carriers), C. H. Severin & Sons Pty. Ltd. (drainage contracting and plant hire), Houlahans Pty. Ltd. (earth moving and construction) and H. A. Robinson (1964) Pty. Ltd. (haulage of sand and bricks). The 'slant' of the combined operation as planned is plain to see; but unfortunately the collapse of the mining boom has left to the urban West a legacy of depression from which there is yet no sign of recovery. In these conditions, contracting businesses such as Steels—and they are not alone—are in the toils and their future is not secure.

In the East Steels first chanced their arm in 1969 by entering into partnership with a newly established Melbourne insurance broking company; Steels' contribution to the venture being that their 'domestic' business would be channelled through the new company. Since then the partner has been bought out. The scale of business written is still small, but the alliance in the United Kingdom of the insurance businesses of Steels and Cayzer Seear Limited must in due course 'brush off' overseas and, in this sphere, Steels should be in Victoria to stay.

In the Canadian chapter, the role of the horse and cart is manifest in the early

Premwire, Melbourne, Australia. Part of Kilsyth workshops

Vinyl Calendering Unit, Sydney, Australia

story of the brothers Pitkethly. In Melbourne, an old photograph of the staff of Premier Wire Works Ltd. includes, suitably off-centre, a "horse and wagon which was the company's sole goods-carrying vehicle in 1933". Even if there be no other common thread between the two, here is further reminder of the kind of 'grass roots' launching of enterprise that future historians seem likely to seek in vain. The steam rollers of chain store and supermarket have all but done their work.

Premwire, as the company has now become, was founded in 1922 as a backyard partnership between Herbert Alexander Chesterfield and Charles Greenwood. Their most valuable assistant then and until her retirement in 1970 was Mrs Chesterfield, who outlives her husband's death in 1963. Greenwood left the partnership after some years, at which time the company was described as "jobbing wire workers", the main effort of the business being the manufacture by hand of wire frames for lamp shades—a product still being made, but by a process now that effects simultaneously 120 separate cross welds in a fifth of a second.

With the growth of the enterprise, the back yard progressively gave place to a factory at Richmond, two miles from the centre of Melbourne. The move was made during the world-wide depression of the early thirties, and existence hung for a while on diversification into the manufacture of kitchen ware, and a windfall order of half a million dish mops when the local subsidiary of Lever Brothers, in a move to boost sales, decided to give away a dish mop with each bar of soap sold.

By 1939 the staff had increased to about eighty and, during the war that followed, star shell parachutes used in the North Sea and at Alamein were Premwire products. By the end of the war a hundred and fifty people were engaged, *inter alia*, in making parachutes ranging from man-dropping to tiny sonar buoy types. Another—and unique—development was the overlay of a thin coating of tin on copper detonator cups to prevent the premature explosion of shells and mortar bombs.

Since the war, Premwire have opened a manufacturing plant for the production of display media and another for the production of wood turnings. They are also engaged in the manufacture of motor vehicle components in a modern factory at Kilsyth, with ample space for further expansion and concentration of activities, and the Richmond base is being run down. The staff now numbers over three hundred, and the variety of manufactured products is too lengthy and too diverse to be listed. The present writer, in his role as Accountant to one of Melbourne's leading schools, can certify to the fact that Premwire's activities now extend even unto the requirements of education in Australia!

Expansion of the order described inevitably called for finance, and Steels acquired a majority interest in Premwire during the final months of this story of a hundred years. A marriage of convenience it may have been but, in a nationally awakened Australia, a shot-gun wedding it was not. Premwire retains its Australian identity.

As this brief Australian chapter closes, negotiations with the owners of the Sydney firm of Michael Nairn & Co. (Australia) Ltd., manufacturers of floor coverings, have borne fruit; and the expansion of Steels' interests into New South Wales looks like being a subject for a future chronicler.

CHAPTER X

THE UNITED KINGDOM

I, who am known as London, have faced stern times before,
Having fought and ruled and traded for a thousand years and more;
I knew the Roman legions and the harsh-voiced Danish hordes;
I heard the Saxon revels, saw blood on the Norman swords.

These are the opening lines of Greta Briggs' war-time verse, 'London under Bombardment', to which General Wavell acknowledged his indebtedness at a time when all looked dark for his North African command. If they seem to dwarf Steels' century to the compass of a novitiate, at least they serve to emphasize the depth of the well from which the company's roots have been nourished. Those roots indeed were Scottish, but the greenhouse was 'the City'; and, to the man under the distant teak tree, 'London Office' was ever a mystic utterance.

In the opening chapter of this story there are brief descriptions of Steels' first and second London bases, respectively at No. 6 East India Avenue and No. 6 Fenchurch Avenue. To those who gazed incredulously on the rubble of the latter, when they arrived for work on the historic Monday that followed its destruction, there was extended promptly the hand of friendship that so unforgettably was the hall-mark of war-time London. On the second floor of No. 61 Threadneedle Street, the staff of The North British & Mercantile Insurance Company moved over to provide space for the refugees from Fenchurch Avenue and the collection of fire-blackened, water-stained objects that had been their files and records.

Nearly a year later, at No. 24 Lombard Street, broader pasture was provided by the Royal Insurance Company, who made two complete floors available to Steels. These were old friends and, while the new City was a-building, Steels were to spend fifteen years as their tenants. Finally, as some may have thought, they moved into the newly-built 'Chesterfield House' at 26/28 Fenchurch Street. This was virgin territory indeed, for the floors of the new offices were surfaced, and the Boardroom panelled, with East African hardwoods from the stands of Steel Brothers (Tanganyika Forests) Ltd. It was an imposing home.

However, the potential for damage of the wood-worm of inflation was soon to make itself felt. By 1968 it had become demonstrable that the annual rental of space to accommodate a waste-paper basket far exceeded the price of the article

London office after destruction by the "Luftwaffe"—1941

Sondes Place, Dorking, with Milton Heath in background

itself. The Scottish roots rebelled against the City greenhouse, and the move to the present headquarters at Sondes Place in rural Surrey was the breathtaking result. Before proceeding further, it may help if we tabulate the caravanserai enumerated thus far—

1873 to 1887—No. 6, East India Avenue, London
1887 to 1941—No. 6, Fenchurch Avenue, London
1941 to 1942—No. 61, Threadneedle Street, London
1942 to 1957—No. 24, Lombard Street, London
1957 to 1969—Chesterfield House, 26/28 Fenchurch Street, London
1969   —Sondes Place, Dorking, Surrey

Sondes Place and a neighbouring manor house, Milton Heath, combine to provide Steels with ample office accommodation and thirty acres of freehold property, of which it is written—"It is possible to look up from one's work and see a deer picking its dainty way across the lawn, or an inquisitive fox foraging at the edge of the trees. Squirrels abound, while the really patient naturalist who is prepared to stay late and walk softly may be rewarded by the sight of a family of badgers in the woods behind Milton Heath." Here indeed is magnificent rejection of the concrete jungle in favour of a return to Nature.

In Steels' Burma days, the London Office, below the level of the Boardroom, was to a great extent the handmaiden of the East. Here were chosen and trained the Assistants to be sent overseas. Here were invoiced the rice, teak and other shipments that came to Europe. Here were procured and despatched the mechanical requirements of mills, mines and oilfields. Here were undertaken multifarious missions of enquiry, acceptance and delivery, all of them having an Eastward slant.

However, there can be no perfunctory dismissal of the role of the Boardroom in the story of Steels. If earlier chapters have conveyed any glimpse at all of the stresses and strains, the decision taking and the heart searching that lie between the lines, then speculation there must be of the qualities of the nine men who, during a period of a hundred years, carried the burden of Chairmanship. The tenth took over as the hundred years drew to its close. They are to be listed as follows—

	Service as (a) full-time executive (b) Chairman of Steel Brothers & Co. Ltd.		Died
William Strang Steel	1870–1908	1890–1897	1911
Hugh Alexander Laird	1870–1906	1897–1906	1911
Sir Robert McCracken	1873–1924	1906–1924	1924
Sir James Duncan	1877–1926	1924–1926	1926
Bertrand Theodore Petley	1900–1930	1926–1930	1930
John Andrew Swan	1898–1940	1930–1940	1940
James Kilgour Michie	1905–1965	1940–1960	1967
Percy George Graham Salkeld	1915–1965	1960–1965	1974
William Francis Graham Salkeld	1920–1970	1965–1970	
James Harold Gaunt	1933–	1970–	

(The apparent absence of a Chairman earlier than 1890 is explained by the fact that until that date Steels were a partnership. They were incorporated as a limited company in 1890. 1970 saw the formation of Steel Brothers Holdings Limited, of which, in a non-executive capacity, William Salkeld became the first Chairman until he retired completely in 1971. James Harold Gaunt, his successor in 1970 as Chairman of Steel Brothers & Company Limited, then assumed the dual role.)

William Strang Steel has already had some introduction. The Strangs and the Steels were notable border reiver families constantly involved in battles on the debatable lands of the Scottish/English border. Their union is implicit in the family name. William acquired the family seat of Philiphaugh in Selkirk, which today is the home of his eldest grandson, Sir William Strang Steel, Bart.

Steel's Far Eastern service, to the extent that it pre-dated the establishment of his own company, has already been described; and his influence is strongly to be read into the shareholding arrangement yet to be explained.

Of Laird, who had a small estate in Perthshire, there is regrettably little on record. His career, from service with Gladstone Wyllie onward to the seemingly premature surrender by Steel in his favour of the Chairmanship in 1897, argues a close bond between the two men. Even the photograph of Laird in the Chairmen's 'gallery' at Sondes Place has been cleverly 'doctored' from an impromptu snap taken during the course of a game of croquet. Nothing more formal could be traced.

Sir Robert McCracken was the son of an Ayrshire farmer of Ardoch in that county—supposedly the *fons et origo* of Steels' telegraphic address 'Ardoch'. He became a man of wealth, and his London residence was in 'Millionaires' Row', Kensington Palace Gardens. Sir Robert was an expert in the field of rice, and his Chairmanship spanned eighteen years. As a personality he was dignified, gentle and quietly spoken. His London day used to start with a homely chat with Walter Frames in front of the general office fire.

Sir Robert suffered from one conspicuous handicap, possibly self-inflicted by reason of holding the reins too long. At his right hand stood one who, perhaps, was the most colourful and dominant personality ever to have strode Steels' stage; and in the later years of his Chairmanship, Sir Robert's was almost a sinecure role.

Sir James Duncan, of Kinnettles in Angus, occupied the Chair for only two years, but his influence had been all-pervading for many more. He was a strong man of few words, his bark worse than his bite. He was human, philanthropic and had a particular sympathy for young Scottish Assistants living in 'digs' in London, particularly if they came of farming stock.

A *Rangoon Gazette* reporter, on the occasion of Sir James' death, wrote—

> Neither my generation nor indeed the generation before my generation knew of Sir James Duncan except as the Man Behind Burma. It's 32 years since he left us, but not yet 32 months since his hand was all powerful in the commerce of the country. Conditions are such now that no man can ever attain Sir James' power—even supposing any other man had the same personality and brain. Which is doubtful.

In London Sir James dominated the commodity markets in Mincing Lane and was the *confidante* of brokers, the Eastern Bankers and the Insurance companies, for he always seemed to be ahead of the news. The stories told about him are legion, and the appendix to this story provided by Ian George Meldrum McGavin (1917–1966) throws further light on a remarkable man.

On his return from Burma, Sir James (then Mister) Duncan bought the estates of Kinnettles and Couper Grange from the Earl of Strathmore, whom his father had served as a ploughman on those self-same lands.

Petley, a forester and a 'Steel Brother' by absorption, as elsewhere described, was a man of great dignity and a staunch churchman. He was the first Chairman who was not a Scot. He had only one eye. It is written of him that he once told a broker seeking to arrange a small tonnage contract that Steels dealt in cargoes not grocery parcels. Petley is not remembered for any greatness, but that could be due to the massive proportions of the pedestal he was required to mount on the death of his predecessor. His Chairmanship ended with a crippling stroke that left him helpless and legally complicated the appointment of his successor.

Swan was a generous but quick-tempered man, a dude—his dress was always in the height of fashion—a ladies' man, and an enthusiastic owner of race horses. He must be considered as having exercised his Chairmanship with considerable ability under circumstances that were not kind to him. His tenure started during a period of world-wide depression and, during his first year, he had to take the unpalatable step of cutting all salaries by ten per cent. It ended with the Second World War, when no man could have been more concerned for the welfare of staff and their families during the upheaval of evacuation. There is little doubt but that his death in office during the darkest days of the war was brought on by the strain of selflessness and concern for others and by the weight of the burden he bore.

Michie, who occupied the Chair for a record twenty years, must be granted comparison of performance, though not of personality, with Sir James Duncan. No lesser man could have guided—nay driven through—the total diversification that became imperative if Steels were to survive a war that ended with the door to Burma slamming shut. He was a hard man who saw his own point of view with great clarity. His ruthlessness limited his friendships to those who really knew him, and his intolerance of shortcomings in others is something for which he will not be remembered with affection by those who did not reach his sometimes unreasonable standards of efficiency. Yet who would say, of a period of doubt and dismay, that the hammer fist on the Boardroom table was not a necessity, or that the moment did not produce the man? Steels owe much to Michie's determination that the company should not only survive, but grow. Indeed he must be regarded as the architect of the modern Steel Brothers.

The brothers Salkeld, another break—though not by many miles—with the tradition of Scottish leadership, stand too near to the present for objective assessment. Let no more be recorded here than Percy's immense consideration, as General Manager in exile, for his staff beleagured in war-time Burma; and William's distinction in becoming the first Chairman of the Holding Company that has emerged from the rationalisation of recent years.

Something now falls to be said of Steels' shareholding arrangements down the years. Although the partnership of 1870 became a limited company in 1890, the essence of partnership persisted, in a broadened way, to include some fifty of the senior executives.

Though the company's preference capital, largely issued over the years as bonuses to the ordinary shareholders, became freely available to the public, the Articles provided that the controlling equity shares, with two exceptions, could only be held by executives of the company, described thereafter, in their triennial agreements and for other purposes, as 'shareholders'. On retirement, these shareholders were required by the Board to sell their holdings to such executives of the company as were invited by the Board to receive them. Normally they would be men of fifteen or more years' service holding managerial positions; the transfer price was certified by the company's auditors each year on the basis of a specified formula.

This formula price, both buying and selling, was substantially below any predictable open market quotation had there been one. Human nature being what it is, the fact was more likely to be apparent when selling; and the procedure was disputed in the Courts by "Moylan and others (who) claimed that excessive amounts had been written off the value of the Fixed Assets and that the value of their shares to be given up should include the Depreciation Reserve". Judgment went in favour of the company, and His Lordship's concluding remarks included the observation that "there are no drones in Steel Brothers' hive".

There was a further, and beneficial, proviso to the shareholding arrangements which ruled that a half of the equity shares, as far as practicable, should be held by staff resident overseas. The intention here was to disallow Directors and senior staff in London acquiring holdings of an order such as would preclude younger men overseas from building up a substantial interest in the company before their retirement or appointment to a senior position in London.

The two exceptions referred to, and then only to a restricted extent, were the direct descendants of the founding brothers (and, happily, the Steel family continue to retain a small holding) and James Finlay & Company of Glasgow. This latter concession was in appreciation of the considerable assistance that William Strang Steel, when he started his business, received from the late Sir John Muir, Bart., of Finlay, Muir & Co., Calcutta (now James Finlay & Company). James Finlay's own history, anent the opening of their Calcutta branch in 1870, records that ". . . the branch had correspondents in Rangoon, W. Strang Steel & Co., later Steel Bros. & Co. Ltd., a company with which James Finlay & Co. have maintained the most friendly associations." These friendly associations have been maintained ever since, and it is only as a result of Steels' ordinary shares becoming freely available to the public on the re-structuring of the company in its centenary year that Finlays have parted with their special shareholding.

*   *   *

The end of the Second World War, and of Steels' operations in Burma, was followed by a surge towards diversification that was reflected nowhere more strongly than in the United Kingdom. Undreamt of realms were invaded, some with, some without success. Sondes Place itself first featured twenty years before it became the company's head office. In 1948, an association between the industrial research organisation of Mactaggart & Evans Limited and Steels opened the place as a centre of industrial research, to which small firms lacking the necessary facilities could bring their technical problems. Mactaggart & Evans were no 'out of the hat' allies in this venture, for Steels had invoked their help in sundry Far Eastern problems over many years. At Sondes Place were installed first-class testing laboratories, wherein were investigated, *inter alia*, "bricks and buttons, cast iron and concrete, dental fillings and detergents, plastics and pencil leads". The work continues, but with the accent now on the manufacture of specialised electronic equipment and testing machines.

The post-war story of Steels and Insurance is that of the proverbial snowball rolling down-hill, but the origins lie much further back.

In the Far East, for many years, Steels had been Lloyds Agents in Rangoon and other ports. The extent of their own local involvement, in Burma in particular, had made of their domestic insurance portfolio a prize to stimulate the zeal of any underwriter. It is not surprising, therefore, that they acquired the local agency of the many well-known Insurance houses enumerated earlier. The spill-over from Rangoon, then and later, has seen Steels and their Associates established as Insurance Agents in such places as Calcutta, Chittagong, Karachi, Colombo, Aden, Cyprus, Amman and Beirut.

As far back as the early nineteen hundreds, Sir James Duncan had been appointed Chairman of the Board of the Royal Insurance Company in London. The appointment was no sinecure—not to a man of Sir James' calibre anyway— for, at the time, the salaries of the London staff of the 'Royal' were below those of the staff at Liverpool, where the head office was located. It was thanks to the personal intervention of Sir James that the disparity was terminated. No bones were broken, for the association between Steels and the 'Royal' has continued to be close and mutually valuable ever since.

Of London there has been earlier mention of the 'Royal's' succour of a bombed-out staff in 1942. It says much for the inter-company relationship that when, in 1949, Steels decided to enter the business of Insurance broking, the 'Royal' transferred to them a senior executive to take charge of the new department, which thenceforward dealt with all of Steels' insurance requirements in the United Kingdom. In 1958 Steel Brothers (Insurance) Ltd. was formed, and a portfolio of 'outside' insurance business built up. In the same year the new company was elected to Lloyds and acquired the status of Lloyds Brokers. Thenceforward, by merger and by take-over, there has been notable expansion. Steels are now known and respected for their role in virtually all facets of insurance and underwriting, and have opened branch offices in Hull, Bristol, Cardiff and Southampton. Two alliances of several call for special mention.

In 1961 Steels took over the old-established business of S. E. Higgins & Company, whereupon there followed a change of trading name to Steel Brothers & Higgins (Insurance) Limited. In 1963 was formed a separate company, Whittington (Insurance and Finance) Ltd., to expand Steels business in Life Assurance. A year later, in its turn, this company spawned Spire Homes Limited, a property development activity directed to the creation of lower-price-range housing estates in the south east of England. The project prospers.

In 1969, the major reorganisation of Steels' financial structure, earlier referred to, made all the equity available to the public and, further, called for a large increase in the ordinary capital to enable expansion to continue. This was largely provided as a permanent investment of forty per cent of the increased equity by The British & Commonwealth Shipping Company Limited, the owners and managers, *inter alia*, of the Castle and Clan Lines of ships and of many other sea, air and industrial interests around the world. The impact on the Insurance Department was that the British and Commonwealth's insurance broking interests, hitherto handled by their own subsidiary, Cayzer Seear Ltd., were merged on an equal basis with those of Steel Brothers & Higgins under the style of Cayzer Steel Brothers Limited. The ramifications of this union are already world-wide.

From insurance, *pace* the incongruity, we move on to grass. Oblique reference has been made in the Rice Department's story to the transfer from London to Hull of the operations of Carbutt & Co. (1928) Ltd. This company in 1952 acquired a fifty per cent interest in Yorkshire Agricultural Driers Limited, which interest was purchased by Steels in 1968.

A contribution to Steels' House Magazine in 1955 by Henry Ormond Andrews, Y.A.D.'s Managing Director, is prefaced by this starkly informative passage—

> Grass is Britain's most important single crop. Not counting rough grazing, we have some 15,000,000 acres of grassland being utilized in one way or another, whilst the total acreage of other crops is less than 10,000,000, and it must be remembered that this latter figure includes all forms of corn, beans, potatoes, all root crops, vegetables, soft fruit orchards, and sundries such as linseed, rhubarb, kale, etc.

The story continues, fascinating but beyond the limits of what this chronicle can retail, to describe the processes of hay making, silage making and artificial drying in such a way as to confer on grass a significance never suspected by the Saturday afternoon tennis player. More importantly it throws into sharp relief an indigenous feed-stuff rich in proteins otherwise to be imported as oil cake, sunflower seed and so on.

To gloss over failure is to devalue success, so mention must be made of two ventures that did not prosper.

Peterlite Products Limited and Expanded Perlite Limited were twin investments in experimental fields. The one was concerned with the manufacture of transparent heat and chemical resistant plastic sheet for use in high-altitude flying and by the electronic, instrumentation and optical industries. The other handled a class of volcanic lavas described as siliceous glasses or pitchstones, providing the base for a super-grade insulant for both high and low-temperature requirements. Steels' involvement started in 1956, but, though the products were of demonstrable superiority in many respects, the entrenched interests behind the marketing of existing equivalents were too powerful and the investments were disposed of after ten years of hard striving.

In 1820, twelve years before William Strang Steel was born, Henry George Sanders went into business in London as an "Engineer and Manufacturer of Pianoforte Actions". It is recorded that he "had a grim struggle at the beginning of his working life and at times nearly succumbed to his difficulties".

For a hundred and fourteen years the business was conducted by three generations of the Sanders family who, by the end of the nineteenth century, had changed course in favour of the manufacture of collapsible, and rigid extruded tubes such as first became familiar as containers for artists' paints, but now are a general purpose product, commonplace alike beside the toothbrush or inside a T.V. set. After the demise of the Sanders line, the company knew less fruitful days until in 1955, its fortunes were revived by an ex-member of Steels' staff, Thomas Otto Mafeking Pope (1920–1942). Pope it was who, in 1936, had been posted to Palestine as the first general manager of Steels' Haifa rice mill, a project which terminated by sale of their interest in 1947. In 1964, mainly through Pope's influence, Steels acquired a majority interest in the business of H. G. Sanders & Son Ltd. Pope's return to the fold, however, was sadly brief, for he died three months later. Today, at Southall in Middlesex, the company prospers as a provider to the packaging and electronic industries.

From one company that is older than Steels we turn to another. In the *House Magazine* published in Steels' centenary year there appeared the following—

> The marriage occurred recently between a dashing bridegroom who had just celebrated his 100th birthday and a demure (but reasonably well endowed) bride of a mere 108 summers.
>
> This was surely a very suitable match as Peirce Leslie & Co. Ltd. (or PL's as it is almost universally known), the latest addition to the Steel Brothers family, has had many business and personal connections with Steel Brothers over the years. The two companies used to trade in rice shipped from Rangoon to Cochin; for a short time they were associated through the medium of Peirce Baumann & Co. Ltd. in a joint cashew venture in East Africa; Steel Brothers have been PL's cashew agents in British Columbia for a number of years; three brothers of the late Mr. J. C. Howison, who was chairman of PL's from 1944 to 1957, were senior executives of Steel Brothers; and during the last war at least two employees of Steel Brothers from Burma worked with PL's in South India. It is, perhaps, more than a coincidence that the capital structure of PL's and, until fairly recently, the provisions in the Articles for capital to be held by working members, bore a striking resemblance to the corresponding features of Steel Brothers—with of course the same problems arising in recent years. It was therefore a happy chance that Steel brothers were introduced to PL's at a time when both companies were considering ways and means of loosening the shackles of their respective constitutions.
>
> Another link in the chain of coincidences was that the introduction was actually effected by The British and Commonwealth Shipping Co. Ltd. with whom PL's have had a remarkably happy relationship since the end of the last century through their Clan Line agency in Malabar. In the end, so many pieces of the jigsaw have fitted into each other so naturally that we may hope the saga will end, like all good fairy stories, with the Prince and Princess living happily ever after.

The author of the article, to which the foregoing is but a preface, is James Noel Anthony Hobbs, Managing Director of Peirce Leslie & Company, who joined the Sondes Place establishment simultaneously with the merger and who, among his other duties, has since fallen heir to the editorship of the *House Magazine*. It is noteworthy that PL's own centenary story is on record in a book called *Century in Malabar*.

At the end of this story, and qualifying for inclusion by a matter only of weeks, is Becorit (GB) Ltd. of Nottingham. In the aftermath of war, James Edgar Farrow, Becorit's present Chairman, found himself involved in the coal industry in Germany at the behest of the Allied Control Commission. After his return to Britain in 1951 he obtained the agency for Becorit Grubenausbau GmbH of Recklinghausen, Germany, who manufactured mechanical steel pit props for use underground. In 1955 these principals were persuaded to form a company in Britain. There followed a decision to manufacture the props in Britain instead of importing them. Henceforward the story becomes one of expansion, through separate companies, into the manufacture of other equipment for the mining industry; even unto Becorit's pioneering of diesel-powered rail systems for the carriage of men and materials underground, a development in which they now operate successfully and almost alone. In 1970 the diverse elements were unified as Becorit (GB) Limited and Steels acquired control of the business in October of that year, with Farrow continuing as Chairman and with the urge to expand and diversify unabated.

EPILOGUE

This "some account" of Steels' first century is told. If it has occasioned any disappointment—even, perhaps, some turning within the grave—that is a risk that had to be accepted if the end product was to be a reasonably portable and better than dry-as-dust volume, offering some prospect of being read before consignment to the bookshelf as no more than public relations material. The risk is heightened, of course, when only one hand guides the pen.

If the story has value, this should belong to the future; for Time is fast thinning the ranks of those who can argue its merits from personal experience, and is swelling the numbers of those for whom it may provide a shaft of light on their commercial ancestry.

Even in the few years that have passed since 1970, the complexion of Steels has changed with the changing times. The company is fast becoming a multi-national corporation. Fashionably, there are those who proclaim such to be a threat to national aspirations. Others there are who regard the concept of nationalism as requiring some re-assessment. Ours may now be too small a world wherein to accept nationalism as a rational or permissible barrier between people and people.

The author of the next volume of Steels' story must surely face a daunting task. He will be dealing, probably, with material more impersonal and impermanent, and with people for whom service with Steels may be something less than a life-time career. Not impossibly, when one measures the mileage between William Strang Steel's first rudimentary rice mill on the Poozoondaung creek and the automated complexity of such as the lime plant at Kananaskis, he will be involved with Steels' participation in a project in Space. He may well be a scientist, and the product of his literary labours is unlikely to owe much to hours of patient typing. Conservation policy may rule that the pulping of timber play no part in book making. His, indeed, may not even be a book as we know the term.

Speculation, if allowed to run riot, could reduce this present volume to a frail starting point for future chapters: but if the next chronicler can accept it as a suitable hitching post for his own task, it will have served that much historical purpose at least.

APPENDIX A—THE TIME SCALE

```
                                    1870 2  4  6  8  80 2  4  6  8  90 2  4  6  8  1900 2
                                       1  3  5  7  9  1  3  5  7  9  1  3  5  7  9    1  3
```

CHAPTER 2 *RICE*
    BURMA ——————————————————
    THAILAND
    GERMANY
    UNITED K'DOM
    CUBA

CHAPTER 3 *TIMBER*
    BURMA ——————————————————
    GUYANA
    TANZANIA

CHAPTER 4 *OIL*
    BURMA
    INDIA
    PAKISTAN
    UNITED K'DOM

CHAPTER 5 *BURMA*
    IMPORTS ——————————————————
    SHIPPING —————————————
    INSURANCE ———
    COTTON ——
    CEMENT
    TIN DREDGING
    MINING

CHAPTER 6 *ASSAM*—STEELS
    CEYLON—STEELS
            CREASY ·····························
            D/BUTLER······(1847) ·····················
    E. AFRICA—BAUMANN ·················

CHAPTER 7 *MID-EAST*—STEELS
           —SPINNEYS

CHAPTER 8 *CANADA*
    STEELS
    LODERS
    YTONG
    DALES
    PITKETHLY
    JORDANS

CHAPTER 9 *AUSTRALIA*
    STEELS
    PREMWIRE

CHAPTER 10 *UTD. K'DOM*
    EXPORTS ——————————————————————————
    INSURANCE
    Y.A.D.
    SANDERS······(1820)······························
    P. LESLIE······(1862) ···································
    BECORIT

N.B. Dotted lines indicate ope

or to association with Steels.

STEEL BROTHERS GROUP ILLUSTRATED IN A "FAMILY TREE"

AT 1st NOVEMBER 1970

STEEL
BROTHERS
HOLDINGS
LIMITED

UNITED KINGDOM

Associates

Attock Oil Co. Ltd.
New General Rice Co.
  Ltd.
Yorkshire Agricultural
  Driers Ltd.

Subsidiaries

Carbutt & Co. (1928) Ltd.
Walter Holmes Ltd.
H. G. Sanders & Son Ltd.
Sondes Place Research
  Laboratories Ltd.
Steel Brothers Under-
  writing Agencies Ltd.
Spire Homes Ltd.
Peirce Leslie & Co. Ltd.
Whittington & Johnston
  Contracting Ltd.
Becorit (G.B.) Ltd.

Subsidiary
STEEL
BROTHERS
AND
COMPANY
LIMITED

Associates

UNITED KINGDOM

Braithwaite Steel Brothers
  (Insurance Brokers) Ltd.

AUSTRALIA

Cayzer Steel Brothers and
  Harlock Pty. Ltd.

Subsidiaries
& Sub-Subsidiaries

Cayzer Steel Brothers Ltd.
Cayzer Steel Brothers
  Home Ltd.
Steel Brothers & Higgins
  (Insurance) Ltd.
P. B. Swain & Co. Ltd.
Wooland & Co. Ltd.
Warren & Partners Ltd.
City Insurance Facilities
  Ltd.
George Burrows Group
  Insurance Ltd.
Whittington Insurance &
  Finance Ltd.
Citadel (New Forest) Ltd.
Cayzer Steel Brothers
  Overseas Ltd.
Steel Brothers & Higgins
  (Middle East) Ltd.
Cayzer Irvine & Partners
  Ltd.
Cayzer Leigh & Co. Ltd.

Associate
CAYZER,
STEEL
BROTHERS
HOLDINGS
LIMITED

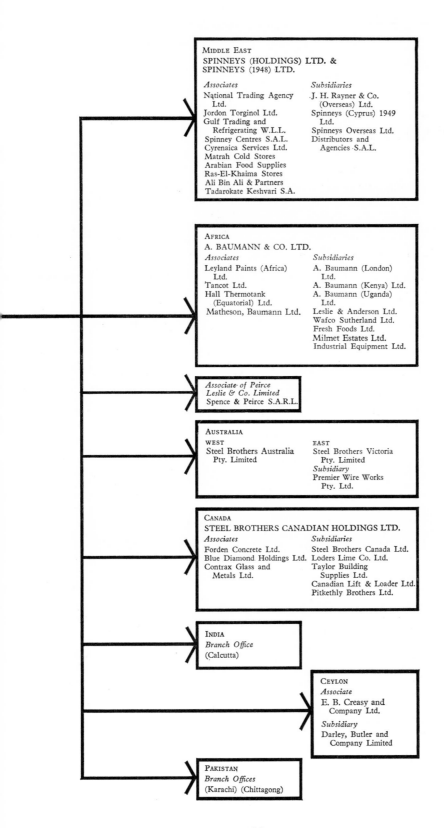

MIDDLE EAST
SPINNEYS (HOLDINGS) LTD. &
SPINNEYS (1948) LTD.

Associates	*Subsidiaries*
National Trading Agency Ltd.	J. H. Rayner & Co. (Overseas) Ltd.
Jordon Torginol Ltd.	Spinneys (Cyprus) 1949 Ltd.
Gulf Trading and Refrigerating W.L.L.	Spinneys Overseas Ltd.
Spinney Centres S.A.L.	Distributors and Agencies S.A.L.
Cyrenaica Services Ltd.	
Matrah Cold Stores	
Arabian Food Supplies	
Ras-El-Khaima Stores	
Ali Bin Ali & Partners	
Tadarokate Keshvari S.A.	

AFRICA
A. BAUMANN & CO. LTD.

Associates	*Subsidiaries*
Leyland Paints (Africa) Ltd.	A. Baumann (London) Ltd.
Tancot Ltd.	A. Baumann (Kenya) Ltd.
Hall Thermotank (Equatorial) Ltd.	A. Baumann (Uganda) Ltd.
Matheson, Baumann Ltd.	Leslie & Anderson Ltd.
	Wafco Sutherland Ltd.
	Fresh Foods Ltd.
	Milmet Estates Ltd.
	Industrial Equipment Ltd.

Associate of Peirce
Leslie & Co. Limited
Spence & Peirce S.A.R.L.

AUSTRALIA

WEST	EAST
Steel Brothers Australia Pty. Limited	Steel Brothers Victoria Pty. Limited
	Subsidiary
	Premier Wire Works Pty. Ltd.

CANADA
STEEL BROTHERS CANADIAN HOLDINGS LTD.

Associates	*Subsidiaries*
Forden Concrete Ltd.	Steel Brothers Canada Ltd.
Blue Diamond Holdings Ltd.	Loders Lime Co. Ltd.
Contrax Glass and Metals Ltd.	Taylor Building Supplies Ltd.
	Canadian Lift & Loader Ltd.
	Pitkethly Brothers Ltd.

INDIA
Branch Office
(Calcutta)

CEYLON
Associate
E. B. Creasy and Company Ltd.

Subsidiary
Darley, Butler and Company Limited

PAKISTAN
Branch Offices
(Karachi) (Chittagong)

123

APPENDIX C

Shipping in the Port of Rangoon on 17th March 1886

Date of arrival	Vessel	Flag	Cargo and destination		Tons	Shippers
1885						
Aug. 17	Russia	British	Rice	Europe	1951	Zaretsky Bock & Co.
1886						
Jan. 4	Gareloch	,,	,,	,,	1177	R. & J. Q. Rowett
,, 28	Machrianish	,,	,,	,,	1699	W. Strang Steel & Co.
Feb. 8	Industrie	German	,,	,,	1642	Diekmann Barckhausen & Co.
,, 9	Corryorechan	British	,,	,,	1998	W. Strang Steel & Co.
,, 11	Isabel Browne	,,	,,	,,	1287	R. & J. Q. Rowett
,, 11	Thunderbolt	,,	,,	,,	1193	W. Strang Steel & Co.
,, 12	Glenesslin	,,	,,	,,	1743	R. & J. Q. Rowett
,, 13	A. E. Killam	,,	,,	,,	1032	Kruger & Co.
,, 14	Wilhelm	German	,,	,,	1315	Bulloch Brothers & Co.
,, 14	Glencairn	British	,,	,,	1564	Mohr Brothers & Co.
,, 23	Kate Thomas	,,	,,	,,	1693	W. Strang Steel & Co.
,, 27	Dunbritton	,,	,,	,,	1471	W. Strang Steel & Co.
Mar. 1	Volta	Italian	Timber	,,	643	B.B.T.C. Ltd.
,, 2	Maria Teresa	,,	Rice	,,	980	The Pegu Co.
,, 2	Giuseppina Bertello	,,	,,	,,	1268	W. Strang Steel & Co.
,, 4	Sherborne S.S.	British	,,	,,	1181	Mohr Brothers & Co.
,, 4	Wodan S.S.	German	,,	,,	1280	Mohr Brothers & Co.
,, 6	Pemptos S.S.	,,	,,	,,	1541	Arracan Co. Ltd.
,, 6	Clydebank	British	,,	S. America	863	R. & J. Q. Rowett
,, 7	Connaught Ranger	,,	,,	Europe	1153	Arracan Co. Ltd.
,, 7	Ambassador	,,	Unfixed		692	Finlay Fleming & Co.
,, 7	Elizabeth Rickmers	German	,,	,,	1246	Kruger & Co.
,, 8	Moidart S.S.	British	Rice	Europe	865	Mohr Brothers & Co.
,, 10	Totos	Norwg.	,,	,,	719	Kruger & Co.
,, 10	Acapulco	German	,,	,,	549	Diekmann Barckhausen & Co.
,, 10	Arracan S.S.	British	,,	,,	1855	Bulloch Brothers & Co.
,, 10	Britannia	Norwg.	,,	,,	653	Kruger & Co.
,, 10	Giuseppa Anna	Italian	,,	,,	1099	W. Strang Steel & Co.
,, 13	Matador	German	,,	,,	1438	Mohr Brothers & Co.
,, 15	Strathblane	British	,,	,,	1364	Arracan Co. Ltd.
,, 15	Firth of Solway	,,	,,	,,	1245	W. Strang Steel & Co.
,, 15	Ruthwell	,,	,,	,,	1296	Bulloch Brothers & Co.
,, 15	Mona	,,	,,	,,	1945	R. & J. Q. Rowett
,, 15	Carl	German	,,	,,	958	Bulloch Brothers & Co.
,, 15	Recco	Italian	,,	,,	759	The Pegu Co.
,, 15	Tagus	British	,,	,,	1242	Mohr Brothers & Co.
,, 15	Dacca	,,	,,	,,	1067	Arracan Co. Ltd.
,, 15	Abydos S.S.	,,	,,	,,	1069	Bulloch Brothers & Co.
,, 15	Levenka	German	,,	,,	437	Diekmann Barckhausen & Co.

Total Tons   48272

APPENDIX D

Being random extracts from Steel Brothers' Forest Department Standing Orders compiled in 1912 and revised in 1932.

GENERAL No. 10.

Exploration Notes.

In reviewing the girdling and exploration reports, that came to hand for last season's work it is noticeable that in all cases there has not been a full appreciation of the extreme importance of thorough exploration. It must be again impressed on all concerned that the whole value of our forest concessions *is wrapped up in girdling. A tree passed over is lost to us for the currency of the lease, possibly for ever, and thorough exploration is the keynote of our getting the fullest possible return*; any failure to obtain such a result must make itself felt by every individual member of the Forest Staff. For Unclassed Forests we have to rely absolutely on our own records for all estimates of their timber worth and such depend entirely on exact and *thorough* exploration. So long as there exists in any of our forests a single square mile about which we lack precise information as to its timber resources, thus long are we unable to obtain a full return for our outlay. Even if an area is not due for girdling for a number of years hence, reliable information is nevertheless wanted *now* if we are to avoid hand to mouth methods and to assure the most economic rotation of exploitation. It is appreciated that the whole of this cannot be done in one season but it is laid down for guidance that every girdling coupe must be explored out at least a year previous to its date for girdling and, in addition, as much more forest as time will permit. This in the main is being done at present but with the inception of an organized scheme of exploration for every area we desire greater thoroughness in exploration methods. We appreciate thoroughly the efforts of Staff in the past but with the good leavening of experience that now prevails, improved and more systematic results are to be looked for in the future.

Without in any way wishing to be-little the assistance derived from guides and hunters in marking down teak areas, we would like to see far more independent and original work carried out. Native information seldom takes one far afield from beaten tracks, and as is well known, information, especially in Kachin tracts, is often suppressed. The statement that any particular forest contains no teak should never be taken for granted—even if appearance is against it— and it should never be considered as negligible until and as a result of personal investigation. Where the native guide can be employed to best advantage is on advance reconnoitering work. The casual volunteer is not the stamp of man to be of value but rather the "mokso" in the pucca sense of the word in preference to the village pot hunter. The real hunter will roam the jungle for long periods at a time away from the beaten track. This class of man ought to be attracted to our employ and given a roving commission to explore out of the way corners where no one in an ordinary way would ever penetrate. This should be his sole duty and when required he would naturally attach himself to any other exploration operations on hand.

*　　*　　*

GENERAL No. 11.

Girdling Operations.

All marketable trees of the fixed minimum girth and above found in the annual block must be girdled.—This in effect throws the onus of finding these trees on the Firm's staff, and too much importance cannot therefore be attached to the systematic exploration and mapping of areas before girdling operations are commenced. We lay it down as a standing instruction that every block must be thoroughly explored a year before it falls due for girdling. This is to say, every tree overlooked in the area may be *lost to us for ever* as girdling will not again be undertaken over the same ground for many years to come. The possible loss which this entails is very great, not only in the *value* of timber outturned, but in the *quantity* which it will be possible to extract for any given area, if quality is found to be inferior owing to a deficiency of First Class girdlings in outturn. We cannot therefore too strongly impress on Assistants all this implies, and the importance that will in future attach to *systematic search for, and production of every tree it is possible to girdle*. Whenever it is possible to girdle a good tree of prescribed dimensions that tree is ours by right under the lease and Assistants accompanying girdling parties should tactfully press for its inclusion. If refused a note should be made of the locality and the Girdling Officer's reasons recorded for declining to girdle *and be reported to the Agent immediately*. We shall be compelled in our own interests to refer these cases to higher authority until the position now conceded by Government is recognised and fully worked up to by local Girdling Officers.

*　　　*　　　*

GENERAL No. 14.

Note on the treatment and work of elephants.

1: *Duty of Mahout.*—The Mahout should start early, say about an hour before sunrise, to follow up his elephant and should observe whether excrement and urine have been healthy and regular and if possible how many times the animal has slept during the night. One "bed" is a normally healthy sign. Two and more "beds" or the absence of any "bed" at all, are indications of something being wrong, as also if the animal has been known to sleep during the day. The Mahout should report to the Singoung anything he has observed in this way immediately on return to camp. He should also at the beginning and end of the day's work report to the Singoung any sores or injuries his animal may have and these should be examined by the Singoung before allotting the work of the elephant for the day.

Frequent changes of mahouts are *very* detrimental to the elephants and must be avoided. It is of the utmost importance to select mahouts of experience and even temper. A highly trained elephant will quickly sink to the level of an ignorant mahout and be just as useless. Many good beasts acquire a reputation for bad temper or are ruined as workers by bad mahouts.

The controlling staff should be on the alert also to see that elephants are in reality liberated in good grazing ground after the day's work or after a march. It is not uncommon for an unprincipled mahout to tie his animal up at night-fall to save trouble in tracking the beast next morning. One wonders then why an elephant falls off in condition and is listless for no apparent reason; and the explanation is probably easily found *viz:* that the beast is half starved and is not obtaining food under natural conditions at night for an elephant is essentially a nocturnal animal. A little vigilance on the part of Assistants and Singoungs should make this sort of thing quite impossible, the signs of it being patent more often than not to an observant eye about the camp and in the forest. In the unfortunate event of an elephant falling from exhaustion or being found "bed ridden" from inability to rise through weakness or some other cause, *the first thing* to do is to give the animal a stimulant.

Then get it on to its feet *at once* and into a natural position; if necessary thereafter bracing it up to the nearest tree with belly bands until strength is recovered. The failure to take these measures promptly will invariably result in the death of the elephant, for it cannot for some reason, recover strength in a recumbent position. An animal that has been "down" should be carefully watched for a day or two after or even tied up until normal physical strength is recovered and it can be safely left to follow its own devices.

*　　　*　　　*

Working hours.—On cool cloudy days during the rains and in the cold weather, elephants in good condition may be safely worked up to 3 or 4 o'clock in the afternoon with the usual intervals of rest *if good fodder is within easy reach*. Special care should be exercised on hot days and especially during the months of September/October and during the May/June start of the new season. Start work then early and knock off about noon on sultry or very hot days if working in shady forests, earlier if in the open. See that a willing dragger is not over tasked and urged to a point beyond his strength. The weekly rest days should be decided upon by the Assistant and not left entirely to the discretion of the Singoung, who may have more than the usual days off, if not properly checked. A good singoung should readily be able to gauge the capabilities of his elephants and tell more or less if an animal is "slacking". Change the task as frequently as possible alternatively on the same or following days for dragging on light and heavy timber. If circumstances compel a long stretch of work on heavy timber or in dragging from stump off hills or the elephant has been worked to exhaustion, give it the necessary day or days rest to recover. In other words gauge the capabilities of the elephants under your charge as carefully as you would a valuable horse and use them accordingly.

In some respects they are most delicate but given decent treatment and with due regard to condition, an elephant will ordinarily stand as much work as most animals employed on hauling. The surest way of success lies in the care of the *individual animal* and that is the reason why a native contractor with one or two elephants is usually able to show a better result than the bigger employer.

5: *Rest Camps.*—When elephants are off work for a season, place them in the best grounds for young fodder obtainable. See that they get a good long "bathe" morning and evening and are thoroughly well scrubbed *all over* with a bath brick or "doh nwai". The bath is especially beneficial during the hot season.

Animals with an "apoo" should then be regularly doctored with medicated tamarinds or native "kasaw" mixed with rice or paddy and salt.

It is more essential at this time that an elephant should be groomed and cared for as carefully as any domestic animal for he will no more readily recover from the effects of hard work or ill health than one's horse would, if turned out of the stables to fend for itself. It is a mistake to suppose the elephant is returning to altogether natural habits in a rest camp for his range is limited. He is still fettered and largely dependent on the care and diligence of his keepers to pick up again.

*   *   *

GENERAL No. 15.

Standing Instructions regarding Elephants.

Hospital Camps. In districts where there are a sufficiency of beasts to warrant the establishment of such, permanent hospital bases may be maintained. Sites selected should be on high, well drained ground with an ample variety of fodder in the immediate neighbourhood, as also good water and shade. All elephants suffering from anything more than a mere temporary ailment of small import should be drafted into a hospital camp. All such ailments as debility, bed abscesses, etc., can usually be much better treated in a hospital camp than in working centres.

Infectious Diseases. The two principal infectious diseases to be contended against are Anthrax and Haemorrhagic Septicaemia—both equally deadly. No known cures are of value in either case and measures to be adopted are therefore only preventive. In the case of either *diseases breaking out or being suspected immediate segregation of healthy beasts* should be adopted and in moving animals in segregation camps it is always advisable to move *up* stream. In limited areas animals should be tied up.

In Haemorrhagic Septicaemia an outbreak is generally considered over ten days after the last case, but animals should not enter an infected neighbourhood for at least a month. or longer if possible.

Anthrax outbreaks as a rule are over about fourteen days after the last case. No term can however be fixed to the period that animals should avoid an infected area as sites of graves, post mortems, etc., retain infection for many years. Careful disinfection of the grave and surroundings must be adopted as well as the erection of a permanent barrier around the grave. Thereafter the immediate vicinity of the grave should be avoided at all times.

On no account should a post mortem be held on the carcass of any animal if there is the least suspicion of death having been due to an infectious disease, as the opening of the carcass increases the spread of disease germs.

APPENDIX E

Foreword (to a Government Report) by Geoffrey Walsh, Esq., Food Controller
and Economic Adviser to the High Commissioner, Palestine.

The entry of Government into the trading arena is fraught with many difficulties since
the normal machinery of Government is not geared to this particular type of activity; the
tempo is strangely rapid and irregular; the idiom of commerce is unfamiliar and the
chaffer of the market place is confusing (and somewhat frightening) to the average civil
servant. Yet the Government of Palestine, in common with many other Governments, was
compelled by the stress of a world war to embark on trading operations on a large scale,
and to adapt its resources to meet the emergency.

Disruption of the normal trade channels with a consequent danger of shortage in
consuming centres made it imperative for the allied authorities to institute an increasingly
elaborate system of regulation of all available supplies, Government trading in essential
commodities forming an integral part of the scheme. The Secretary of State for the
Colonies, the Combined Food Board, the U.K. Ministry of Food, the Ministry of War
Transport, the M.E.S.C. and the U.K.C.C. were among those concerned with the problem
of equitable distribution of available supplies (including the most economic use of a very
limited amount of shipping space) to the many countries depending on the allies for their
sustenance and into this intricate pattern the complementary machinery for supply and
distribution of essential commodities to the people of Palestine had to be integrated. Force
majeure thus impelled the local Government into the role of a trader.

In such circumstances it was indeed fortunate that a firm of the high standing of
Messrs. Steel Bros. & Co., was available on the spot to assist the Palestine Government
when war conditions left no option to Government trading, and that adverse conditions
in other parts of the world released a trained staff for service with the Palestine branch
of the firm to cope with the ever increasing range of activity connected with Government
trading in Palestine.

The appointment of Messrs. Steel Bros. & Co. as Government Agents was made in
September 1940 when it was decided that in order to synchronise with the allied supply
plans in respect of a modified form of controlled purchase of bread grains, some streng-
thening of the local machinery of procurement and distribution was necessary. In those
early days of the war the problem of supply was comparatively simple and operation
through normal trade channels in the countries of origin was still possible though
restricted. The Combined Food Board, M.E.S.C. and U.K.C.C. had not yet come into
being and the functions of the Government Agents were limited to procurement of wheat
from overseas suppliers and subsequent internal distribution of these supplies on the
instructions of Government. With the passage of time and extension of the war fronts
the supply position deteriorated with great rapidity and what had been a mild incon-
venience developed into a stern necessity to conserve such supplies as could be obtained.
The external allied control machinery was greatly elaborated and as a corollary the
machinery for control over supply and distribution of supplies for consumption in

Palestine was similarly expanded. It was at this stage that the wisdom of appointing as Government Agents a firm of high standing and side resources for the handling and distribution of Government owned commodities became abundantly clear, and experience proved that such an arrangement was, in fact, essential to the efficient handling of a situation which demanded the existence of an organisation sufficiently flexible and competent to deal as they arose with the many commercial problems connected with the handling of a bewildering range of Government trading activities.

From the comparatively simple business of purchasing wheat on Government account from external sources of supply through normal trade channels, the progressive deterioration in the supply and shipping position necessitated a rapid expansion of Government trading operations through the Agency, and created problems which could not have been foreseen when the Agency was first inaugurated. The system of bulk purchase of cereals (including rice), oil-bearing seeds and sugar through M.E.S.C. and establishment of the U.K.C.C. simplified problems of procurement so far as the Agents were concerned, but difficulties of distribution increased as the range of Government owned commodities widened.

Honey, tinned fish, tea, coffee, pepper, dried eggs, dehydrated meat, milk, potatoes, cocoa-beans and saccharine, not to mention wonder beans (of unhappy memory since even pigs turned up their noses at these so called "wonder beans", the only apparent justification for the name resting on the fact that the Agents ultimately succeeded in disposing of the stock albeit at a heavy loss) in addition to commodities under bulk purchase, were among the foodstuffs handled and distributed by the Agents, who were also required to handle large quantities of potatoes and other vegetables procured by Government from the Levant States under growing contracts, to set up buying centres in Trans-Jordan for the purchase of cereals on Palestine Government account, to arrange for the purchase and distribution of village surpluses as declared under the Palestine cereals crop assessment scheme and to supervise the acceptance and distribution of very large numbers of slaughterstock purchased under contract on Government account.

In the earlier stages of Food Control it was found necessary to acquire some 40 lorries for the transport of Government owned foodstuffs. These were operated by the Agency and in due course became merged in a wider Government Transport scheme involving nearly 500 Government lorries operated by Messrs. Steel Brothers & Co. as a separate branch of the Agency, under the aegis of which a fleet numbering some 1,700 privately owned local lorries was also coordinated to handle W.D. and essential work throughout the country.

The Government Transport Agency was disbanded in September 1945, thirty lorries being retained for the service of Food Control.

This skeleton outline of the multifarious duties undertaken by Messrs. Steel Bros. & Co. as Government Agents gives little indication of the detailed work involved or of the innumerable problems of supply and distribution which required to be, and were, settled on the spot. A more comprehensive record will be found in succeeding pages but the scope of the task may be gauged by the fact that from 1941 to 1945 the tonnage of goods passing through the Government Trading account exceeded one million tons of a value of more than £30,000,000.

Relations between the Government Agents and Food Control (the Department most closely concerned with the bulk of trading operations) have been consistently cordial, and friction has been virtually non-existent. This may be attributed in large measure to the able handling of a competent staff by Mr. T. O. M. Pope, Mr. W. Salkeld and Mr. J. B. Clark, who have successively been in charge of the Agency and I take this opportunity of paying my personal tribute to their successful endeavours which resulted in the detailed handling and distribution of large quantities of foodstuffs over a long period with scarcely a hitch.

The emergency which necessitated establishment of the Government Agency is passing and in due course reversion to peace-time conditions of trade will dim the nightmare problems of procurement and distribution of essential commodities in a world engaged in total war. But so far as Palestine is concerned, the impact of the war was far less severe than in many, if not most, other countries and the Government Agents had no small part in maintaining a comparatively even flow of vital supplies in the most difficult circumstances. For myself, I shall always look back with real pleasure on my association with the staff and firm of Steel Bros. & Co. during my tenure of office as Food Controller of Palestine.

Geoffrey Walsh

FOOD CONTROLLER
ECONOMIC ADVISER
To The
HIGH COMMISSIONER.

12.11.45.

Facsimile of letter dated Rangoon, 20th Sept. 1883, from Mr. (later Sir) Robert McCracken to Mr. William Strang Steel in London.

APPENDIX G

Meeting of Directors –
31st December 1890.

Present.
W.H. Steel Chairman
Jas. A. Steel.
H.A. Laird.
John E. Borland
R. McCracken.
J. McAllan
O. Christien

Approved and signed Minutes of last Meeting.

Considered and formally accepted the proposal of Messrs Steel Brothers & Co London and W. Strang Steel & Co. Burmah to make over to the Company the assets and the liabilities of the said firm as from the 31st December 1890 upon the terms set forth in the form of agreement between the Company and the members of the said firms which has been prepared and upon which the Chairman has endorsed his name for the purpose of identification being the Agreement referred to in paragraph A, clause 3 of the Memorandum of Association with certain modifications thereof which have been agreed to and made therein –

Resolved that the Company shall undertake and forthwith commence to discharge the liabilities of the said firm from the 31st December 1890 as provided by the said form of agreement

Resolved that the seal of the Company be affixed to an agreement in the said form as soon as the Managers may think expedient or whenever the proposed parties thereto the Members of Steel Brothers & Co shall require it

Facsimile of pages I and II of meeting of Directors on 31st December 1890 (on which date the partnership of Steel Brothers & Company became the Registered company of Steel Brothers & Company Limited.)

Authorized Mr Borland on behalf of the Company to send to Messrs Steel Brothers &Co a copy of the above resolutions with a letter requesting them to place the Company in possession of such of the said assets as have not already been transferred to the Company as and when the same are ascertained

Resolved – That the Company do purchase acquire and take on lease from W.Strang Steel the properties mentioned and specified in the said form of agreement as to be purchased, acquired and taken on lease from him upon the terms and for the price and consideration provided in the said form of agreement and that Mr Borland on behalf of the Company write to Mr Steel to that effect and request him, as against the issue to him of the shares provided for in the said form of agreement to hold the said properties according to the respective tenures thereof to be acquired by the Company upon trust for the Company until the necessary assurances and leases shall be prepared for execution by him –

Approved the Agreement marked A as to the issue of shares with £80 paid up thereon intended to be filed with the Registrar of Joint stock Companies – Directed the seal of the Company to be affixed to same

Proceeded to allotment of shares

APPENDIX H

The City of London in 1917

(condensed from the recollections of Ian George Meldrum McGavin (1917–1966))

The City of London, when I joined Steels in 1917, was still strongly influenced by the habits and customs of the Victorian era. It was still quite common to see horse-drawn vehicles and buses with open-top seating on the street. The City was very much a merchant city, dominated by the great merchant houses, the merchant banks and the Eastern or Exchange banks as they were then known. The great joint stock banks were as yet unknown. There were shipping and insurance businesses, the commodity markets and the money market, of which London was the world centre, consisting of the discount and private finance houses.

Steels banked in London with the Bank of Scotland, Parr's Bank (now National Westminster) and the Capital and Counties Bank (now Lloyds). They did much documentary business with The Chartered Bank of India, Australia and China, The National Bank of India (now National & Grindlays), The Imperial Bank of India, The Nederlands Bank and the Hongkong and Shanghai Banking Corporation.

The City of London's reputation for integrity then was perhaps at its zenith. A man's word in business was his bond and there was no need for arbitration or court cases. Failure of contract was amicably settled by the parties concerned, to the mutual credit of themselves and the City.

In Steels' Fenchurch Avenue office, as elsewhere, mechanical accounting machines were unknown. Only heavy typewriting machines were in use, and these were usually operated by men until a desperate war-time need for manpower for the Forces opened the door to female participation in the business life of the city.

In the Fenchurch Avenue office we still sat on tall stools before high, sloping desks with a brass rail above the ridge. On this we put our books of account and everything else so that we had a clear working surface. Telephones—the pedestal type with the receiver hanging on the protruding arm—were scarce, one to a department. Every call had to be put through the Telephone Exchange operator, of whom you requested connection with the number required.

The quiet and peace of Fenchurch Avenue were maintained by a beadle, suitably attired in a long frock coat and a top hat bearing on its side a gilt cockade. He was an ex-cavalry man, and woe betide any messenger boy who came gaily whistling through the Avenue. A kick on the bottom abruptly stopped the tune. The occupiers of the surrounding buildings each contributed an annual sum towards the beadle's wages. His morning cup of tea was partaken behind our hydraulic lift shaft by the courtesy of dear Mrs. Young, our real genuine Cockney housekeeper.

Mention is made elsewhere of the destruction of our Fenchurch Avenue building in the Second World War (when Mrs. Young, among others, was killed). In the First world War we too had three near misses. Apart from infrequent Zeppelin airship raids at night, there were two daylight raids on the City of London undertaken by light German Fokker planes with open cockpits. I remember we youngsters running out into Lime Street Square in time to see the planes just above chimney top height flying over. The airmen were plainly visible and must have heaved the small bombs overboard.

On a Saturday morning I was returning to office after paying in the cheques to the

Bank of Scotland in Bishopsgate. As I turned into Leadenhall Street a bomb dropped close to an Eastern Telegraph Company's messenger boy on a bicycle. As far as I know he was killed. The bomb pierced the asphalt road surface and fractured the water main. The water ran down Leadenhall Street in a flood and took with it the jewellery sucked out of the window of an adjacent jeweller's shop.

Our General Office manager was Walter Mill Frames, a real Pickwickian character if ever there was one. His first action on arriving in the morning was to tear off two foolscap sheets from a scroll pad and paperclip them round the starched cuffs of his shirt sleeves. After the first day the paper covers fitted nicely in place and, for the sake of economy, were religiously put away in his desk drawer overnight for a maximum use of three days. Sam Shelley, the office factotum, once tried to persuade him that they had only been used for two days, but Frames knew from the colour that they had done the required service and off the paper came and into the waste paper basket. You could not fool him!

Frames was a very kindly man, and to every new young member of the staff he used to present a copy of *The Pilgrim's Progress*. Nevertheless there was that in his make-up that made him a frequent victim to leg pulling. One of my earliest recollections is of him greeting a service member home on leave from the battlefields of Flanders in the First World War with the words "I'm glad to see you're back from the front". From the tone in which he said it I was not quite sure whether Mr Frames meant that he could see right through the man or was surprised to find him still alive.

There was a day when Frames, who was very fond of gardening and flowers, brought some narcissi into the office. They were white ones and he put them in a vase on his desk. During the lunch hour, when the office was free of seniors, we dipped the narcissi into red ink so that, when he came back, instead of white narcissi he had brilliant red ones.

Frames, who believed in attending his doctor regularly each week, used to bring up for this purpose a sample bottle to take to Dr. Crosby in Cullum Street quite close to the office. He used to put the bottle on the shelf of a big double-door safe and, during a particular lunch hour, we obtained some saccharin and popped it into the bottle during Frames' absence. Of course, a day later when the sample was analysed, he was told that he had something badly wrong with his urine, and for a week or two afterwards a number of bottles of red medicine were sent into the office for Frames to take.

Frames was a great lover of cats. He simply adored them and would never think of cats being put down by a vet. Whenever one of his cats had kittens he either got someone to take them and give them a good home or else he kept them himself. It was a great sight, when you went to his house in Sidcup, to see a herd of cats wandering about his rockery to the annoyance of the gardener. On a particular morning he came into the office and said to his colleague, Charles Ferrier,—"What do you think, Charles? Richard has had kittens. Would you believe it?"

There was a day when Mr. Petley, the company's fifth Chairman, phoned to say that he would be late coming to the office as there was fog on the Beckenham line. In a typical reply Frames answered—"You're quite right Mr. Petley: there is a fog on the line. I can hardly hear you."

A favourite lunch-time prank was to get hold of the London telephone directory and glance through it until we found a likely name, to whom we would then put through a "suitable" enquiry. Our "victims" ranged from a horse slaughterer in Aldgate to a venerable gentleman in charge of a Lads Brigade. After a time this ploy got risky, for we went a wee bit too far. One day we phoned up Marie Lloyd, the Music Hall star, at her home in Golders Green. The conversation got involved and unfortunately she reported the matter to the police. Enquiries were made and, though they never traced us, it rather put a damper on this lark.

In the days of which I am writing, it will surprise the modern generation to know that the highest salary paid in the London Office was £1000 per annum to the Chairman. The other Directors and the senior managers received a maximum of £500. I actually started as a trainee at £30 a year, which will also stagger the present-day newcomer. However, we managed, with a contribution from home, and really got some kick out of life even on those modest salaries. Sir James Duncan, when he was Chairman, always had his monthly salary paid in cash. It was the practice to deliver salary envelopes simultaneously with the salaries book, which you signed to show you had received the money. Sir James' one twelfth of £1000 came to £83–6–8. On one occasion we withheld the two copper pennies from his envelope, which I delivered to him. He did not, of course, check the envelope immediately, but he signed the book and out I went. I had hardly got back to my desk when Sir James' door opened and a loud voice boomed out "Whaur's ma tuppence?"

When I first entered the portals of Steels, Sir Robert McCracken was still Chairman but, by this time, more in name than in deed. Sir James really ruled the roost. Sir Robert would come in late and start his day with a homely chat with Frames in front of the general office coal fire. He really did very little work, but sat in his office reading the papers until he went to lunch either at the City Club or the Oriental Club. When he returned, Sir James considered that it was time he went home, so he just called out to Sam Shelley, our effervescent Cockney head messenger, "Fetch McCracken a taxi-cab" and he bundled him off.

We had a junior on the staff called Robins, who was a member of the London Scottish Regimental Pipe Band. One day, when all the seniors were away at lunch, he decided to practice on his pipes and so he tuned up and set off marching up and down along the tops of the sloping desks playing away lustily. The rest of us got hold of our round black ebony rulers and acted as drummer boys, drumming away on the tops of our desks. Of course the racket was awful and, unfortunately, Sir Robert returned early from lunch and descended upon the scene. We immediately packed up and got down to our work, but when Frames got back from lunch his bell rang and in he went to Sir Robert's room, where the incident was related to him. Frames thereupon took us all into Sir Robert's room and lined us up in front of his desk like a platoon of soldiers, ready to be strongly admonished by the Chairman. However, at that particular point, Sir James arrived back, saw us crowded in the room with hardly space to move and asked, "What is all this about?" Sir Robert explained that we had been misbehaving ourselves kicking up an awful racket on the bagpipes at lunchtime. Sir James, in his usual abrupt manner, said, "A lot of nonsense, eh? Tell them all to get back to their desks and get on with their work". Then he called Sam Shelley for the inevitable taxi!

There was another incident in which Sam Shelley was involved. It was Sir James' habit to go to lunch either at the Oriental Club, the City of London Club or to the Carlton Hotel, where he resided during the week. (The week-ends he usually spent North in his mansion house at Kinnettles). On a particular occasion he went out without his umbrella which, normally as he left, he would swing in his hand, shouting across the office, "If Lord Inchcape calls tell him I am dining at the City of London Club". Sam Shelley spotted the forgotten umbrella and started off with it in pursuit of Sir James. As he passed along the passage towards the front door, he imitated Sir James by swinging the umbrella and calling out in a loud voice, "If Lord Tom Noddy calls tells him that I am dining with the Archbishop of Canterbury at the ABC". As he was saying this, Sir James, who had returned promptly for his umbrella, was watching and was really amused. He was not angry and could see the funny side. He was that type of man.

We youngsters ran a scratch rugger or soccer team as and when suitable matches presented themselves. Before Sir James left for Euston for his week-end visit to Kinnettles, he would look at the team on paper and suggest changes, which I am afraid we ignored. But the great thing to us was that he gave us a fiver for a meal after the match. That usually meant a great night in the West End of London for, in those days, a fiver was really something.

We have all heard of schoolboy howlers. What of business howlers? Let me quote just one, being a letter from the wife of a member of our saw mills staff asking for sea passages to Burma—

'Dear Sir,
   My husband in Rangoon says you know all about steamers' passages.
   He says you are responsible for my childrens births as well as my own. Last time I had them on the *Leicestershire* s/s. This time I would like to have them on the *Staffordshire* s/s.
   My husband says you know how to fix me in a single cabin so that I can have my children next door.
   Please do your best.
Yours in anticipation'

I felt she was anticipating rather too much!

And what of today? Steels are faced with new problems, but these will be overcome as those in the past were overcome, while the Company goes forward with further developments and fresh ventures.

APPENDIX I

The Directors of Steel Brothers & Company Limited
(since incorporation of the Company in 1890)

	Board	Chairman
William Strang Steel	1890–1908	1890–1897
James M. Allan	1890–1910	
John Ebenezer Borland	1890–1899	
Edward Chrestien	1890–1903	
Hugh Alexander Laird	1890–1906	1897–1906
Sir Robert McCracken	1890–1924	1906–1924
James Alison Steel	1890–1895	
Sir James Duncan	1897–1927	1924–1926
Robert Williamson	1897–1919	
Edward Albert Christian Gibbs	1909–1913	
Bertrand Theodore Petley	1913–1930	1926–1930
John Howard Glover	1920–1939	
James Alexander Toomey	1920–1930	
John Andrew Swan	1924–1940	1930–1940
James Kilgour Michie	1927–1962	1940–1960
Thomas Taylor McCreath	1929–1960	
William Thomson Howison	1930–1951	
Reginald Hugh Lloyd Langford James	1942–1960	
Sir John Tait	1945–1964	
Percy George Graham Salkeld, C.B.E.	1950–1968	1960–1965
Armour McGilvray	1952–1962	
Gordon Stewart Nicoll, C.B.E.	1952–1968	
Kenneth Lockley	1960–1963	
William Francis Graham Salkeld	1960–1970	1965–1970
Charles Henry Elliott	1961–1970	
James Harold Gaunt, C.A.	1963–	1970–
Gerard Wilfred Royds	1963–1964	
Hector William Harben Valentine	1965–1967	
James Taylor Wishart, M.C., T.D., Ll.B.	1967–	
James Alexander Thomson, C.A.	1969–1970	
Dunstable Philip Shan McCarthy, O.B.E.	1970–	
James Godfrey McCulloch	1970–	
James Crawford Purdie	1970–1970	
Alexander McCulloch French	1970–	
Archibald Sneddon McIntyre	1970–	
John Morrison Smith	1970–	
David Ernest William Thomas	1970–	
Nigel Whitehead, M.B.E.	1970–	

BIBLIOGRAPHY

Chapter I

Anon — "Burma 1870–1963": House Mag. Vol. XVII No. 2 1963

Braund, H. E. W. — "The Melody Lingers On": House Mag. Vol. XVII No. 2 1963

Fergusson, B. E. — "Beyond the Chindwin" : Collins, London, 1945
  (Lord Ballantrae) — Foreword to "Distinctly I Remember" by Harold Braund: Wren, Melbourne, 1972

Frames, W. M. — "Early Days": House Mag. Vol. I. No. 1 1939

Hope, P. L. — "The Fourth of January 1948": House Mag. Vol. IV No. 3 1948

Morrison, I. — "Grandfather Longlegs": Faber, London, 1947

Salkeld, P. G. G. — News Letter No. 26 Feb/Apr 1943

Stanford, J. K. — "Never No More": Blackwood's Magazine Nov. 1948

Stiven, G. O. — "Old Times and Old Timers": House Mag.
                            Vol. II No. 3 1940
                            Vol. II No. 4 1941
                            Vol. III No. 1 1941
                            Vol. III No. 2 1941
                            Vol. III No. 3 1941

Times Literary Supplement — "When the Twain did meet": 27th Apr 1973

Williams, J. M. — "No. 6 on the night of 10th May 1941": House Mag. Vol. III No. 3 1941

Woodruff, P. — "The Men Who Ruled India": Cape, London, 1954

Chapter II

"Beloogyun" — "The Paddy Cultivator": House Mag. Vol. I No 3 1939

Cattanach, J. C. — "Clippers and Rice": House Mag. Vol. V No. 1 1949

Clark, J. B. — "Jungle Paddy Buying": House Mag. Vol. I No 4 1940
— "Burma and her Rice Export Trade: House Mag.
                            Vol. III No. 1 1941
                            Vol. III No. 2 1941
                            Vol. III No. 3 1941

Downes-Shaw, R. E. — "The Rice and Paddy Fleet": House Mag. Vol II No. 4 1941

McCracken, J. — "The Loungzats Have Come": House Mag. Vol. III No. 2 1941
— "The Story of Carbutts": House Mag. Vol. VII No. 1 1951

Milne, W. T. — "Early Days in Bangkok": House Mag. Vol. III No. 3 1941

Rawlings, D. A. R. — "An Episode in Cuba": House Mag. Vol. IX No. 2 1953

Salkeld, P. G. G. — "The Burma Rice Trade": 29th June 1928 Company records

Thiessen, M. — "Neue Allgemeine Reisgesellschaft mbH, Hamburg": House Mag. Vol. XX No. I 1968

Van Tent, E. W. — "Van Tent Lifts The Curtain": House Mag. Vol. VIII No. 2 1952

BIBLIOGRAPHY

Chapter III

Anon
— "Rafting Elephants across the Irrawaddy": House Mag. Vol. IV No. 3 1948
— "The Opening of the Houston Sawmill": House Mag. Vol. X No. 1 1954
— "Rondo Report": House Mag. Vol. X No. 2 1954
— "Farewell to British Guiana Timbers": House Mag. Vol. XI No. 1 1955

Bennett, A. F.
— "Langwe": House Mag. Vol. IV No. 3 1948
— "Crabwood through Camaria": House Mag. Vol. VI No. 2 1950
— "Wineperu": House Mag. Vol. VI No. 2 1950
— "Kaieteur Falls": House Mag. Vol. VII No. 2 1951

Carpenter, J. N.
— "Umbrella Men": House Mag. Vol. V No. 1 1949

Edmeades, F. D.
— "A Happy Landing": House Mag. Vol. IX No. 1 1953
— "Cutting a Line": House Mag. Vol. X No. 1 1954

France, F. H.
— "Early Days in the Forests": House Mag. Vol. I No. 1 1939

Ferrier, A. J.
— "The Care and Management of Elephants in Burma": William Lea, London, 1948
— "A Jungle Tragedy": House Mag. Vol. V No. 2 1949

Glass, J. B.
— "Burma Teak": House Mag. Vol. I No. 2 1939

Hartrup, F. H.
— "Stampa": House Mag. Vol. VIII No. 1 1952

Howe, P. A. W.
— "The Mazaruni Rapids": House Mag. Vol. IX No. 2 1953

Hundley, G.
— "How Literacy Came to the Thoungyin Valley": House Mag. Vol. III No. 3 1941

Longhurst, H.
— "The Borneo Story": Newman Neame, London, 1956

Lovett-Campbell, P. V.
— "All in the Day's Work": House Mag. Vol. I No. 3 1939

Lunan, W. A.
— "Reminiscences": House Mag. Vol. VII No. 1 1951

Miller, R. W. R.
— "Visit to the Rondo": House Mag. Vol. VII No. 2 1951

Morley, C. P.
— "The Elephant Hospital": House Mag. Vol. I No. 3 1939
— "A *Tawtha* in British Guiana": House Mag. Vol. V No. 2 1949

Rosner, C. E.
— "Joys of Jungle Life": House Mag. Vol. I No. 3 1939

Wellard, E. K.
— "Memories of the Thoungyin": House Mag. Vol. IX No. 2 1953

Williams, J. H.
— "Elephant Bill": Rupert Hart-Davis, London, 1950

Wright, E.
— "A Journey to Sarawak": House Mag. Vol. IX No. 1 1953

Chapter IV

Anon
— "The Story of Lanywa": House Mag. Vol. I No. 3 1939
— "A Short History of The Attock Oil Company Ltd.": House Mag. Vol. II No. 2 1940
— "The Indo-Burma Petroleum Co. Ltd.": House Mag. Vol. XI No. 1 1955
— "Dhulian Gas": House Mag. Vol. XII No. 1 1956
— "Jubilee Year of The Attock Oil Company": House Mag. Vol. XVII No. 1 1962
— "If at first you don't succeeed": House Mag. Vol. XX No. 2 1969

Braund, H. E. W.
— "Golden Jubilee 1963": The Attock Oil Co. Ltd., London, 1963
— "Distinctly I Remember": Wren, Melbourne, 1972

Carne, J. N. — "Ten Years' Development in The Punjab": House Mag. Vol. VI No. 1 1950

Darling, W. — "I.B.P.'s Darling": House Mag. Vol. IV No. 3 1948

Dunsire, T. — "Old Timer": House Mag. Vol. IV No. 3 1948

Harman, J. B. — "The Beginning of a Great Development": House Mag. Vol. I No. 4 1940

Lindsay, H. J. M. — "Letter from Chauk": House Mag. Vol. VIII No. 2 1952

Lodhi, T. A. T. — "The Deepest Well in Pakistan": House Mag. Vol. XII No. 2 1956

McCreath, T. T. — "Teething Troubles of the I.B.P.": House Mag. Vol. II No. 3 1940

Mitchell, J. — "My Early Days in The Punjab": House Mag. Vol. X No. 2 1954

Musgrave, T. F. — "Looking Backward": House Mag. Vol. III No. 1 1941

Pinfold, E. S. — "The Fight Against Malaria at Indaw": House Mag. Vol. II No. 3 1940

Polglase, E. B. J. — "To search for Oil and Gas in the United Kingdom": House Mag. Vol. XVII No. 1 1962

— "The Search for Oil and Gas in The U.K.": House Mag. Vol. XVIII No. 1 1964

Rendall, R. — "Forty Years Afloat": House Mag. Vol. VIII No. 1 1952

— "The Last Voyage of S/S *Shwedagon*": House Mag. Vol. IX No. 1 1953

Russell, H. B. — "A Master Mariner Harks Back": House Mag. Vol. XIX No. 2 1967

"Spunyarn" — "A Grand Old Ship": House Mag. Vol. II No. 4 1941

Tun Shwe — "Lanywa": House Mag. Vol. VIII No. 2 1952

Chapter V

Anon — "A Short History of Consolidated Cotton & Oils Mills Ltd.": House Mag. Vol. II No. 1 1940

— "The Story of The Burma Cement Company": House Mag. Vol. IV No. 2 1947

— "Strand Hotel, Rangoon": House Mag. Vol. V No. 1 1949

Bennett, A. F. — "The Old and The New (or Elephants reconstruct B.C.C., Thayetmyo)": House Mag. Vol. V No. 2 1947

Bennett, G. D. — "A New Boy looks at Thayetmyo": House Mag. Vol. IX No. 1 1953

Braund, H. E. W. — "Steelmine": House Mag. Vol. I No. 4 1940

"Distinctly I Remember": Wren, Melbourne, 1972

"Casey Terite" — "Prospecting in Burma": House Mag. Vol. II No. 1 1940

Chapter VI

Anon — "A. Baumann & Co. Ltd.": House Mag. Vol. VII No. 2 1951

— "A Short History of E. B. Creasy & Co. Ltd.": House Mag. Vol. VIII No. 1 1952

— "Assam Notes": House Mag. Vol. XIII No. 1 1957

— "Baumann's Cold Store": House Mag. Vol. XVI No. 1 1960

— "Assam Notes": House Mag. Vol. XVII No. 2 1963

— "Colombo back in the News" House Mag. Vol. XX No. 2 1969

Astell, G. H.   — "Cocoa from Ceylon": House Mag. Vol. XII No. 1 1956

Dunbar, U. B. H.   — "Assam Notes": House Mag. Vol. VI No. 1 1950

Frisby, F. J.   — "Tea in Ceylon": House Mag. Vol. XI No. 1 1955

Langley, W. K. M.   — "Century in Malabar": Madras, 1962

Shaw-Hamilton, C. F.   — "Assam Notes": House Mag. Vol. VI No. 2 1950

— "Assam Notes": House Mag. Vol. X No. 2 1954

"Tea Time": House Mag. Vol. XVIII No. 1 1964

Chapter VII

Anon   — "Palestine Post": House Mag. Vol. IV No. 2 1947

— "Palestine News": House Mag. Vol. IV No. 4 1948

— "Palestine Chatter": House Mag. Vol. V No. 1 1949

— "Aden—A New Venture": House Mag. Vol. X No. 1 1954

— "Vale Palestine Branch": House Mag. Vol. X No. 2 1954

— "British Trade Fair at Baghdad": House Mag. Vol. XI No. 1 1955

— "Aden": House Mag. Vol. XII No. 1 1956

— "Supermarket in Beirut": House Mag. Vol. XIX No. 1 1966

— "Spinneys in Muscat & Oman": House Mag. Vol. XIX No. 2 1967

Bridle, A. J.   — "Libya": House Mag. Vol. XVII No. 1 1962

Lockley, M.   — "Middle East Impressions": House Mag. Vol. XIV No. 1 1958

Polglase, E. B. J.   — "Spinneys (1948) Limited": House Mag. Vol. XVIII No. 1 1964

Shipton, G. M.   — "Cyprus Calendar": House Mag. Vol. IV No. 4 1948

— "The Gulf of Akaba": House Mag. Vol. IX No. 2 1953

Warren, R. S.   — "Spinneys in the North Sea": House Mag. Vol. XVIII No. 2 1965

Chapter VIII

Anon   — "The Chairman's Visit to Canada": House Mag. Vol. X No. 2 1954

— "News from Canada": House Mag. Vol. XI No. 2 1955

— "Canada Notes": House Mag. Vol. XII No. 1 1956

— "Alberta Ytong Ltd.": House Mag. Vol. XII No. 2 1956

— "The Pitkethly Story": House Mag. Vol. XII No. 2 1956

— "A Brief History of Dales Bros. Ltd.": House Mag. Vol. XIII No. 2 1957

— "Pitkethly Brothers Ltd.": House Mag. Vol. XV No. 1 1959

— "The First Rotary Lime Kiln in Western Canada": House Mag. Vol. XX No. 1 1968

— "Blu Chip": House Mag. Vol. XXI No. 1 1970

Jordon, M. E.   — "Loders and Kananaskis": House Mag. Vol. XIII No. 1 1957

— "Mining at Loders": House Mag. Vol. XIV No. 1 1958

Muir, G. D.   — "Loders Lime Company Ltd.": House Mag. Vol. X No. 2 1954

Reesor, L. R.   — "From Canada": House Mag. Vol. XX No. 2 1969

Chapter IX

Anon — "The Australian Family Continues to Grow": House Mag. Vol. XX No. 2 1969
— "The 'Gen' from Western Australia": House Mag. Vol. XXI No. 1 1970

Bridle, A & A — "Spinneys Acquire New Interests in Western Australia": House Mag. Vol. XX No. 1 1968

Gipton, N. J. — "Premier Wire Works": House Mag. Vol. XXI No. 1 1970

Houlahan, L. — "Houlahans Pty. Ltd.": House Mag. Vol. XX No. 2 1969

Chapter X

Anon — "Sondes Place Research Institute": House Mag. Vol. VII No. 2 1951
— "London Office": House Mag. Vol. XIII No. 1 1957
— "Steel Brothers Insurance Ltd.": House Mag. Vol. XIV No. 1 1958
— "Open Day at Sondes Place Research Institute": House Mag. Vol. XIV No. 2 1958
— "H. G. Sanders & Son Ltd.": House Mag. Vol. XVIII No. 1 1964
— "Spire Homes Ltd.": House Mag. Vol. XIX No. 1 1966
— "Sondes Place Research Institute Exhibit Their Wares": House Mag. Vol. XX No. 1 1968
— "Yorkshire Agricultural Driers Have a New Look": House Mag. Vol. XX No. 2 1969

Andrews, H. O. — "Yorkshire Agricultural Driers Ltd.": House Mag. Vol. XI No. 2 1955

Blattner, A. — "What is Perlite?": House Mag. Vol. XV No. 2 1959

Frames, W. M. — "Early Days": House Mag. Vol. I No. 1 1939

Hobbs, J. N. A. — "Peirce Leslie": House Mag. Vol. XXI No. 1 1970

Jeffrey, J. G. A. — "Opening of Sondes Place Research Institute": House Mag. Vol. IV No. 4 1948

Langley, W. K. M. — "Century in Malabar": Madras, 1962

McGavin, I. G. M. — "Some Memories of the London Office": House Mag. Vol. XIX No. 2 1967

Ross, M. — "Peterlite Plastics": House Mag. Vol. XVII No. 2 1963

Underwood, G. C. — "Steel Brothers & Higgins (Insurance) Ltd.": House Mag. Vol. XVI No. 2 1961

GLOSSARY

*of Asian words not to be found in
the Shorter Oxford English Dictionary*

Bur — Burmese   Urdu — Urdu

Bhatti (Urdu)	A lamp
Bo-gyi (Bur)	A big chief
Burra sahib (Urdu)	much as *Bo-gyi*
Chaung (Bur)	River, creek (alt. School)
Chukka (Urdu)	A period of play (orig. polo)
Dah (Bur)	A long-bladed knife
Dukan (Urdu)	A shop
Galone (Bur)	A rebel or bandit
Hsaya (Bur)	A teacher
Khud (Urdu)	Ditch, ravine (usu. roadside)
Loonzain (Bur)	Lightly milled rice
Loungzat (Bur)	Large river craft
Mali (Urdu)	A gardener
Nat (Bur)	A spirit
Ngapi (Bur)	Rotted fish
Oozie (Bur)	An elephant rider
Oung (Bur)	To shove with the forehead
Pejeik (Bur)	Unmounted helper to *oozie*
Phongyi chaung (Bur)	A monastery
Punkah (Urdu)	A fan
Singaung (Bur)	An elephant foreman
Tawtha (Bur)	A peasant
Taungthu (Bur)	A hillman
Thakin (Bur)	Master (honorific)
Thin-bon-gyi (Bur)	A reading book
Twin-za (Bur)	A well owner

INDEX

145

Soc ✓
HF
497
B7
1975